D1345752

MICHIGAN STATE UNIVERSITY
LIBRARY

MAR 0 3 2014

WITHDRAWN

GUIDANCE MONOGRAPH SERIES

SHELLEY C. STONE

BRUCE SHERTZER

Editors

75E-2.60

GUIDANCE MONOGRAPH SERIES

The general purpose of Houghton Mifflin's Guidance Monograph Series is to provide high quality coverage of topics which are of abiding importance in contemporary counseling and guidance practice. In a rapidly expanding field of endeavor, change and innovation are inevitably present. A trend accompanying such growth is greater and greater specialization. Specialization results in an increased demand for materials which reflect current modifications in guidance practice while simultaneously treating the field in greater depth and detail than commonly found in textbooks and brief journal articles.

The list of eminent contributors to this series assures the reader expert treatment of the areas covered. The monographs are designed for consumers with varying familiarity to the counseling and guidance field. The editors believe that the series will be useful to experienced practitioners as well as beginning students. While these groups may use the monographs with somewhat different goals in mind, both will benefit from the treatment given to content areas.

The content areas treated have been selected because of specific criteria. Among them are timeliness, practicality, and persistency of the issues involved. Above all, the editors have attempted to select topics which are of major substantive concern to counseling and guidance personnel.

Shelley C. Stone

Bruce Shertzer

PSYCHOLOGICAL EDUCATION IN THE ELEMENTARY SCHOOL

RICHARD H. KICKLIGHTER
GEORGIA DEPARTMENT OF EDUCATION

HOUGHTON MIFFLIN COMPANY · BOSTON
ATLANTA · DALLAS · GENEVA, ILL. · HOPEWELL, N.J. · PALO ALTO

BF
77
.K48

ISBN: 0–395–20061X

Library of Congress Catalog Card
Number: 74–12516

COPYRIGHT © 1975 BY HOUGHTON MIFFLIN COMPANY. *All rights reserved. No
part of this work may be reproduced or transmitted in any form or by any
means, electronic or mechanical, including photocopying and recording,
or by any information storage or retrieval system, without permission in
writing from the publisher. Printed in the U.S.A.*

CONTENTS

B503773

EDITORS' INTRODUCTION

Within the past few years several specialists within the field of counseling and guidance have introduced and written extensively about psychological education, its desirability, its value, and its application in the schools. It encompasses many types of activities and is described by the Guest Editors of the *Personnel and Guidance Journal*'s May 1973 issue as "... carefully designed courses that inculcate mental health and personal adjustment. It is a new curriculum area in which people learn to understand themselves and more effectively get what they want." For the school counselor, psychological education implies a new role conception and altered functions.

Richard Kicklighter's monograph focuses on psychological education at the elementary school level. The rationale behind psychological education, its methods, and the means of programming it are thoroughly covered. Dr. Kicklighter's monograph is richly laced with samples of curricular materials and approaches to implementation of psychological education.

For the reader who seeks an understanding of an exciting innovation in the field of counseling and guidance and who seeks to know not only what it is but also its methods and uses, this monograph is essential reading. The author has done an outstanding job in producing a very readable and informative resource of value to practitioners and students.

Shelley C. Stone
Bruce Shertzer

AUTHOR'S INTRODUCTION

William James said, "There is a time in the life of the child to fix a skill." One of the skills that needs to be "fixed" in the life of every child is the ability to know and to understand him/herself and others. To live effectively and fully, all of us must learn to know our feelings and emotions, our fears and hopes, our conflicts and frustrations. Without the skills of living given by such knowledge, many children will be denied the chance to live the "good" life.

Children can learn skills of living. They can come to know themselves and why they behave and feel as they do. They can be armed with the knowledge of living that will give them a real chance to use their abilities to the fullest. The schools are critical in the determination of the acquisition of behavioral skills. What happens in the school is probably society's most important single controllable variable. What we do to and for children will, by and large, determine how they will live. And that is what this monograph is all about.

RICHARD H. KICKLIGHTER

1

The Need for
Psychological Education

It should not be necessary to document the need to strengthen our efforts to support programs of psychological education for children. Indeed, a cursory look around his or her professional house should convince the most skeptical educator that something needs to be done. Any given teacher can point to two, four, or even more children in the class who are not learning, who are disruptive and hostile, or who are withdrawn and sad. If the teacher's memory is sharp, he or she can remember a number of former students who later dropped out of school, or who are now in jail, on welfare, or in a mental hospital. He or she can remember the chronically sad boy who is now the adult alcoholic or the fearful withdrawn girl who became a social recluse. Evidence of the disabling conditions of childhood and the relative inability of the educational enterprise to deal constructively with them abounds. Think your way down your own street in your own home town. How many children do you know personally who are misfits in school, in their families and their neighborhood?

Eli Bower's (1969) studies indicate that there will be an increase of 116 percent in mental hospital admissions of 10- to 14-year-old children in the period 1965–1973. Further, he estimates that an additional 250,000 children are seen for treatment at mental health clinics and another 500,000 are brought before the courts each year on delinquency charges. Bower cites studies that confirm the fact that as many as ten percent of our school-age children have significant learning, emotional, or behavioral problems and that at least two percent are in acute need of help.

Further documentation of the shocking situation relating to child mental health was reported by the Joint Commission on Mental Health of Children in 1973. The Commission estimated that one third of all children under the age of six live in homes that are at or near the poverty level. Of course, poverty itself creates for the child a high risk of later manifestation of disturbance in school. The Commission goes on to say that eight to ten percent of all school children have emotional problems severe enough to warrant special attention. This would mean that about 2.7 million elementary school children in this country have significant emotional disorders. In addition, there are approximately 110,000 children born each year who are mentally retarded.

Poverty and Education

The significance of such a large number of impoverished and retarded children lies in the high risk these children have of suffering from behavioral and learning problems. The Commission reports that about one third of such children are seen by their teachers or by mental health specialists as having emotional difficulties that interfere with their development. Another third are seen as having at least transient emotional problems.

Research has clearly established the strong relationship between poverty and subsequent difficulties in school achievement, physical and mental development, and disabling mental and emotional problems. The literature in this area is vast. However, for a flavor of the scope of the problem the reader may want to review the work of Riessman and his associates (1964) and Hollingshed and Redlick (1958).

Children who do well academically in school, by and large, are able to use the school environment successfully to fulfill their social and emotional needs. As Bower (1962) points out, "achievement probably precedes all other factors as a basic factor in school success." He goes on to say that "realistically, there is increasing ... evidence to support the hypothesis that children who find healthful satisfaction in relationship with family, neighborhood, and school will, as adults, find these same satisfactions." Bower (1965) concludes that, "by the same token, failing children become failing adults."

This conclusion is in accord with the social competency model of development which is based upon attention to ego processes of the human organism as the key to fostering good adaptive behavior in human beings. For too many years our attention has been focused on the intrapsychic processes of the individual with scant attention given to the outcomes of those processes. This means that we have ignored competency in children as a *goal* of education and instead have treated competency as an *outcome* of unspecified educational activities and extraneous psychological processes. Now it is suggested that we deliberately attend to the development of social and emotional competencies in children so that the emotional processes and intrapsychic developmental stages will be automatically in phase as the child matures.

Positive and Negative

For too long we educators have accepted the fatalistic notion that we can only do as well as the limitations or potential of the material (i.e. the children) will permit. "What can you do?" is the common lament we hear. "Look at his home situation!" Unfortunately, this kind of resigned logic gives us an excuse for our failures; we rarely accept our successes so modestly. Our bright achieving kids are products of our educational program and processes! The facts are that we can enhance the development of the bright, well-motivated child and that we can improve significantly the functioning of the less well-endowed. The educational experience is a powerful force in the shaping of the developing personality, and we must accept the situation as one offering equally great possibilities of success or abysmal failure. *What we do in schools for and to children is critically important to their social, emotional, educational, and vocational development.* In one important study on the effects of the educational experience on children, Richard and Katherine Gordon (1963) found some disturbing facts:

> The records of 174 private psychiatric outpatients in New Jersey were studied in an effort to learn whether the patients' difficulties were related to educational strains. Here are the percentages of a group of young male patients for whom, it was reported, the stresses of getting an education were the primary reasons for seeking psychiatric help:

> | | 1953–55 | 1956–57 | 1958–59 | 1960–61 |
> |---|---|---|---|---|
> | Aged 13–24 | 34% | 54% | 56% | 74% |

> Stresses related to education drove nearly three-fourths of the youthful patients to psychiatrists' offices in the 1960's as compared to only one-third in the early 1950's. Certainly, other problems are upsetting

today's youth . . . worries about jobs, about military service, about nuclear war. But the majority of teenagers and young adults who sought psychiatric help blame their troubles on the strain of getting an education.

Accepting the premise that the child who is not doing well at school is in the high risk category for potential emotional disorder, we need to turn our attention to the kinds of problems in children that make them susceptible to these difficulties. But first we need to consider briefly at least an alternate argument regarding cause and effect in certain learning and behavior disorders of childhood.

Competency and Concepts of Worth

We have said earlier that children who do well in school feel good about themselves and develop successful ways of relating to their environment. Similarly, we have stated that children who fail in school also are unsuccessful in building suitable self-concepts and subsequent satisfactory adjustments to their life situations. But let's reverse the cause-effect relationship for another look. Suppose we accept that children who feel good about themselves are able to successfully cope with school demands as well as life's circumstances. Hamachek (1969) says that "Increasing evidence indicates that student failures in basic school subjects as well as the misguided motivation and lack of academic involvement characteristic of the underachiever, the dropout, the culturally disadvantaged, and the failure may be due in part to unhealthy perceptions of the self and the world."

The question, then, is "do we teach social competency skills and develop fully functioning children?" or "do we teach psychological competencies and positive affect and develop fully functioning children with positive social competencies?" We probably need to attempt to do both. There really are no compelling or logical reasons why most academic content cannot be made to serve both purposes simultaneously.

At any rate, we do know that certain children are more likely than others to develop disruptive social and emotional problems during the course of their school lives. We know for instance that economic poverty has little to commend it either educationally or psychologically. As we have seen earlier, at least one third of children from poverty-ravaged families show persistent problems in school learning and adjustment.

Intellectual deficit is another risk factor for maladjustment. Approximately three percent of the children in our schools can be classified as mildly or moderately retarded (Kirk, 1972). The task that these children face in developing adequate modes of coping with their educational environment is formidable. Behavioral and social problems are frequent concomitants of mental retardation.

Children who are neglected, abused, or forced to lead disruptive lives with alcoholic or disturbed parents are extremely vulnerable to later life stress, both in and out of school. So are children whose homes are shattered by death, divorce, or desertion. Children who have other learning or living handicaps will be represented in disproportionate numbers among those with adjustment difficulties in later life. This includes children with physical impairments, speech difficulties, and chronic health problems. And last, but far from least, are those children who have been variously labeled as having specific learning disabilities, perceptual handicaps, minimal cerebral dysfunction, Strauss syndrome, hyperkinetic disorder, or whatever. These children are particularly prone to the development of later-life adjustment problems because of their failure to succeed in developing literacy skills in school. Often, they are seen as bright and able students but as negative, stubborn, destructive, and unmotivated. The contribution of school failure to the later-life problems of these children is all too obvious.

Our grading practices contribute in no small way to the potentiality of motivation and learning problems for children. Most grading schemes are relatively based so that achievement is judged to be adequate or inadequate based on the mean attainment of the group. This approach to child evaluation means that the top half of any given group of children will be judged as doing well academically while the bottom half is not. It is easy to see that the brighter child is more likely to be rewarded for his/her school work and to increase his/her feelings of esteem and self-competency while the slower child (for whatever reason) is likely to have to settle for a grade that is unsatisfactory to his/her sense of worth and competency. This pressure for achievement (i.e. a grade), with parental, peer, and school rewards and punishment attendant on what you "get" on your report card, is probably the single most anxiety-provoking and emotionally disruptive factor in the schooling process.

Lisa's Report Card

Let's follow Lisa, an eight-year-old third grader, on report card day. Lisa comes from a poor but hard-working family. Her mother finished high school and works as a clerk at the checkout counter of a food store. Her father dropped out of school in the eighth grade.

He works as a laborer in construction. Lisa's parents want her to have a "good" education. They want her to have a better chance and a more fulfilling life than they have had.

But, there's a problem. Lisa is far from the brightest child in her room; in fact, she's a bit slow. She's in the bottom reading group and although she's working diligently and hard, she and her group are just now finishing the reading books at the second grade level, while the top group is beginning fourth grade level work. Lisa gets mostly C's on her report card. Many of her classmates get A's, a number of them get B's and only one or two get D's.

"What did you get on your report card, Lisa," smiles Mary. "I got nearly all A's. Let's see yours."

"It's none of your business," whispers Lisa grasping the folded card tightly. "I get A's too when I try. I just don't always try hard."

Mother comes home tired from the store. While she's preparing supper, she remembers it's report card day. "Lisa, where is your report card?" Lisa looks up from her TV program. "We didn't get it today." Lisa tries this ploy tentatively. "Come on now Lisa, I know you got your report card. Where is it?" Mother sounds grim.

After a solemn, slow, agonizing inspection of the record, Mother sighs. "Lisa, you could do better than that. I'm disappointed in you. You promised you would try harder." Lisa sits with her head bowed.

Benign Neglect

We can only speculate about the multiple effects of this kind of scene played out over and over again in homes throughout the country. But we can see some of the effect of this sad little drama in later dropouts, destructive and disruptive school behavior, psychosomatic illnesses, school phobia, and saddest of all, in defeated, unmotivated children.

Obviously, school organization and practice can be improved to the distinct advantage of the psychological well-being of the child. Many progressive school systems have made substantial progress in such things as grading practices. It's ironic that one of the biggest hurdles to the reform of grading procedures is overcoming the resistance of the parents of the school children themselves.

Numerous attempts have been made by enlightened educators to make grading/evaluation processes more meaningful and less stressful for children and parents. Various "combination schemes" involving comparisons between ability and achievement or ability-achievement-effort have been tried but usually with limited success. Written descriptive reports on child progress coupled with interviews are probably the most realistic and useful ways to accomplish the purpose of a productive communication between school and parent. But even this process is resisted by parents. It is time- and effort-consuming, and it is not as precise as the spuriously supposed accuracy of the grade scheme A, B+, B, or the even more deceiving numerical grade 96 or even 91.7!

Parents resist this more enlightened, less threatening procedure. "I want to know just what he is doing," they say, meaning that they want to see a report card with a grade on it just as they had when they went to school. Some educational processes are forgotten soon after the student leaves his/her class; others linger forever. It's sad that so often it's the peripheral, superficial side-effects of the educational experience that seem to persist in our memories, feelings, and behaviors. We never forget the sickening feeling accompanying a failing grade on our report card.

The clientele of the school obviously includes the parents of the children enrolled. One of the tasks of the school is finding ways to help children receive the support and approval of their parents. It is not enough to help children find satisfying, self-enhancing experiences unless we can help their parents to see the results as positive. Helen Hefferman (1966) describes how school organization can contribute positively as well as negatively to this purpose:

> Many parents express dissatisfaction with the child and the school if their child is not in the top reading group or is not accepted in the program for the gifted. The parent, aware only of his own desires or expectations for the child, structures goals which demand certain types of performance, behavior, and achievement. When these expectations are not compatible with the abilities of the child, both school and child suffer from parental disapproval. Even though the child may have done his best, he cannot escape the feeling that he has disappointed his parents by not measuring up to the standards they expected of him. The ultimate effect of unrealistic expectations can only be defeatism. The child or youth who might have been a happy, well-adjusted person making a valuable contribution to his community in some work suited to his capacity may become one of life's failures — a statistic in society's heavy burden of the mentally ill.

It seems clear that the schools must accept two basic philosophic beliefs as the basis of their planning and operations. The first is that the school experience is a powerful force, positive or negative, in the development of the child's social, emotional, vocational, and intellectual competencies. Second, it seems to be clearly established that "benign neglect" is an insufficient operational attitude for the schools to adopt toward most children. Without deliberately designing and implementing a positive, growth-enhancing educational experience, many children will be social casualties in their homes and families and handicapped as adults in their later lives. The goal of the school is obvious and the task is visible to all who would look. However, the means to the accomplishment of the end, fully functioning children, is not so easily determined or described. In subsequent chapters we will see how some people have attempted to cope with this job.

The Whole Child Revisited

Many centuries ago Socrates advised his contemporaries to "know thyself." His followers probably paid as much attention to his advice then as we do today, which is to say, not a lot! Verbally, we accept his admonition as important, but our behavior betrays the fact that we don't accept it as something that is important enough to actually put into practice. We still act as if *what we know* is more critical to our lives and living than *how we feel.* Yet, when we speak frankly and openly to each other, we readily acknowledge that the essence of our being is in our sense of worth, our feelings of belonging, our common affective relationships with those we value, and our comfort in a secure place in our work and with our friends and family. We know the real quality of life is in effective, productive, pleasurable relationships with others. Few could claim that the ability to solve a quadratic equation, to conjugate a Latin verb, or to recall the price of the Louisiana Purchase has had any appreciable impact on the quality of their lives.

Feeling and Knowing

Earl Kelley (1965) says that what is critically important is how we direct and control our behavior, and this depends not so much on what we know as on how we feel. He points out that one can be a saint or a demon with similar funds of common knowledge. The critical issue is one's ability to open oneself to the feelings and needs of others and to relate these to onself and one's goals. Because of this complex interaction between knowing and feeling, it really is impossible to deal with one without affecting the other. Learning does not occur in an affective vacuum nor does feeling develop in the absence of experience. In this regard then, what we learn in the schooling experience is an inextricable part of how we come to feel about ourselves and our world. Kelley (1965) states, "Subject matter and feeling are so closely intertwined that they can no longer be considered a duality. Everyone who learns something has some feeling about it, and so, as in so many other areas, they are inseparable. No matter what we do, affective learning goes on anyway. When this affective learning is positive, the learner becomes constructive in his behavior."

Yet, we deny formally and operationally what we so freely admit in our living every day. Educators are living a schizophrenic professional existence! Our verbal behavior and our often-stated beliefs are simply not compatible with what we actually do! Our schools' curriculum structure and content, instructional techniques and procedures, and saddest of all, our student evaluation practices are predicated on the assumption that what we know is more important than what we are. "You are what you know" might be one way of phrasing the motto of the current educational enterprise.

We must accept the obvious conclusion that human beings are irrational animals. They must be. At least, we educators, counselors, and psychologists must be! We stand back in professional horror and try to catch the rejects from an ill-conceived system that regards and treats a child like a computer to be programmed and informationally armed rather than like a developing human with needs for nurture, care, growth, and fulfillment. Like the nursery keeper, we need to be concerned with the *conditions of growth.* Unlike the grocery clerk, we should not be concerned with keeping the educational shelves and bins filled with a preselected quality and quanity of goods that we *think* people need.

Educators simply cannot do very effectively what they have tried to do for so many years. They cannot select, package, and program behaviors and knowledge and instill their system in the behavioral repertoire of a human being. It won't work and by now we should know how really unsatisfactory that process is. Education, when viewed as a humanistic rather than technological process, is a matter of providing the conditions and the skills that foster growth. How much water (content) does the plant need, and in what amounts (structure) and how often (scheduling)? How warm (organization) must the hothouse be, and what kind of fertilizer (success experiences) must the plants have? Careful attention must be given to pruning and trimming (family involvement) and to control of disease and pests (special help and treatment).

Human beings can, in effect, be programmed and, to a degree, trained. Sometimes these procedures are desirable and useful, as when we are teaching a psychomotor skill or working with an autistic, head-banging child. But, in a real sense, humans must be developed, they must and will grow. Like the nursery keeper, we need to know what kind of environment our charges need for healthy, vigorous growth.

Decartes said, "I think, therefore I am" and by his words excited generations of philosophers and intellectuals. How much more appropriately he might have said, "I feel, therefore I live."

"The Whole Child"

Is there an educator alive who hasn't heard the phrase "the whole child" and who hasn't responded finally with feelings of resignation if not downright nausea? It's the shibboleth of modern schooling, the password to the brotherhood, the incantation chanted by generations of prospective teachers, counselors, psychologists, and other pupil personnel workers. Our negative reaction to the phrase is probably occasioned by our awareness that we don't give credibility to our words. For purposes of understanding, the whole child can be divided into two parts. He/she is a physical being and a mental being. And it is here that our comprehension of child development apparently ends. If we give the child a course in health and provide a physical fitness program, that takes care of one half of the whole child, right? Then we add the three R's, along with other necessary knowledges and content, and we cover the other half of the whole child. Right? Wrong! We have flunked simple division!

The second half of the whole child (mental) is also divisible into two parts. In the interest of simplicity, we can label those parts intellectual and emotional. Without consideration of the relative value of the parts of this whole child we can see arithmetically that one fourth of our child is made up of affective "stuff," or feelings and emotions. And while it is true that the affective life can develop from its spontaneous experience with knowledge and conceptual processes, it is also true that the fullest development of this sphere of human life can never occur without specific attention to its nurture. It will develop spontaneously and naturally, but it should be, in addition, a planned, guided development.

There are at least two excellent reasons why we must give specific attention to the affective development of the child in the educational process. The first and most obvious is that content learning and skill development are inextricably meshed with feelings, motivation, and aspirations. Children who see themselves as inept and incapable don't learn effectively or quickly. Children whose energies are consumed by anxieties, worries, and threat have very little left to give to the task of reading or writing or computing. Children who expect to do poorly, by and large, will do poorly. The aspirations of the child who has experienced only failure and frustration will be a constricting, limiting, and debilitating drag on his/her efforts to make sense out of schooling. If for no other reason, we must attend to the psychological needs of the child so that he/she can attend to, understand, and use the content and skill training that the school provides. Regardless of our attitude toward the responsibilities of the school, a depressed, anxious, frustrated child with a negative view of him/herself and his/her abilities makes a very poor student.

Groups and Peers

To make the most effective use of the school experience, the child has to learn how to be a part of a group. (S)He must learn that cooperation and respect of his peers will help him in his struggle to become an achieving student. He needs to know that pleasure-giving encourages pleasure-receiving and that his lot will be easier and more enjoyable if he can elicit behavior from his teacher that is characterized by helpfulness, patience, and concern.

So, even the most traditional, conservative school faculty has to be concerned about the emotional life of their students even if their only goal is to produce high academic achievers. Introducing sound psychologically based instructional techniques into the regular program of studies so that affective and instructional goals are complementary is certainly an important step in the direction of enhancing the growth of the "whole child."

A second and more compelling reason to be concerned about the "feeling" child relates to the pervasive quality of the affective nature of all humans, including children. Everything we touch, or do, or think, or see, or hear, or believe, or experience is accompanied by feelings. Emotions are the essence of any and every experience. How we feel is how we are. Enhancement and development of affectivity is essential to the realization of the qualities of humanness that make us "people" and not just another animal species. When we have forgotten every fact that we ever knew and every skill that we ever learned, we can still relish the awareness of the feelings we have for the joys and sorrows we have lived.

Life and Feeling

The affective substance of human life should be the major focus of our efforts in educating the child. Nobody ever committed suicide for not being able to understand *Silas Marner*, although some may have suffered because their selves were demeaned for failing to learn it! No stomach ulcers were ever generated for want of the knowledge of a second language. Few jobs have ever been lost because of inability to understand and explain *Hamlet*. But many productive, fulfilling lives have been lost because of anxiety, hostility, uncooperativeness, and conflict. Feeling good about oneself will be an effective influence on one's behavior long after facts, skills, and knowledge are forgotten. Unfortunately, so will bad self-feelings.

Now, this is not an attempt to depreciate or devalue the acquisition of knowledge and skills. Obviously, a major educational task for the school lies in equipping its students with literacy skills, providing a background of cultural understanding, and preparing children to cope with social, economic, and vocational tasks. But, these goals can be accomplished in emotionally satisfying ways and through psychological techniques and programs that enhance the self-concept of the learner. However, content teaching utilizing psychologically desirable methods alone is not enough to enable schools to maximize their profound developmental responsibilities. Direct teaching of an affect-loaded curriculum as a part of school offerings is essential if children are to become "fully functioning" beings.

A "New" Curriculum

This curriculum will include content relating directly to the major psychological developmental needs of children. It will include material on such topics as understanding feelings, understanding others, fear and anger, values and choices. It will be based on the developmental needs of children as we know them from the available research (McCandless, 1967). It will encompass many different kinds of techniques, methods, and procedures utilizing all the available technology and maximizing the varying skills of all staff members in the schools. It will be an organized, developed, specified curriculum with detailed goals and explicit evaluation procedures. As Ivey and Alschuler (1973) put it, "Eclectic procedures systematically organized to teach a specific outcome are more effective than single procedures used to solve a variety of problems."

Do we really need to do something different from what we are doing now? Fred Wilhelms and a host of others believe we do. Describing the student in today's schools, Wilhelms (1972) says,

> look underneath the sometimes bizarre posturings, the gluttony for sensation, the apparent hedonism, and if my eyes do not deceive me, you are looking at a generation in distress; a generation torn by doubts, disgusted with dog-eat-dog materialism, imbued with a vague

idealistic vision of what our wealth ought to make possible, assailed by fears of an ominous future, depressed by a feeling of helplessness, in a massive impersonal, manipulated society, and yet sure they must and can take charge of it. They move from one fad to another, whether in drugs or sex or politics. They often look ridiculous.

All of the Child Comes to School

Our commitment to the sound and fruitful development of the child must include consideration of all of the child if our ability to use effectively what we know now is to be realized. Whether we like it or not, we must deal with all of the child. Though we may limit our aspirations to the academic and literacy growth of a child's skills, we cannot, without severe penalty, ignore the fact that the task is dependent on attention to all the parts it subsumes. Children come to school with feelings, emotions, motivations, and aspirations. They see themselves as relatively capable humans or as inept failures, and further growth is predicated on these critical attitudinal variables. The massive and vitally important report of the Joint Commission on Mental Health of Children (1973) stresses the futility of ignoring the affective nature of the learner:

> Learning is incomplete from the developmental view unless it encompasses both cognitive and affective domains and utilizes the forces — the cumulated meanings, feelings, wishes, conflicts — of the inner life of impulse and affect; it is essential that children have opportunity to express feelings directly in their relations to people in school; it is essential that they have opportunity to re-express indirectly, in symbolic form, the affective elements of their encounter with the outer world.

Magnitude of the Job

One of the major difficulties one has in attempting to organize and discuss meaningfully the topic of psychological education in the schools is the sheer weight, depth, and breadth of the available and pertinent literature on the subject! Professional journals, which have multiplied like amoebas, are replete with articles and research papers on some aspect or other of the topic. As the reader will see, there are packaged programs available, curriculum guides, lessons and unit plans, films and filmstrips, and a host of appropriate media materials to complement teaching efforts. The substantive books that deal directly with the general subject area are great in number. The major difficulty in effectively furthering the advance of psychological education lies in organizing, codifying, and classifying competing and complementary theories, plans, and programs, and bringing some categorizing light on the present state of existence of the field.

Classification and organization will contribute to the further development of affective education for children. There is little doubt that this will help considerably. However, the primary barriers to further extension of an affect-based curriculum for children lie in the attitudes, beliefs, and experiences of educators themselves. Until college professors of education, school administrators and teachers, counselors and psychologists, and school social workers are truly convinced that it is appropriate, useful, and essential that affective education be offered to the developing child, the efforts and programs we have read about and described will remain as tentative suggestions, clever ideas, innovative beginnings, investigative projects, or in many cases, as efforts of the "way out" crowd to worm their way into the "system."

Bower (1965), one of the most effective and proficient writers and thinkers on the subject, says that effective development of psychological education is retarded because the "experts" feel that no internal changes in what we do will be really effective without a thorough overhaul of the social-economic structure of our environment. In addition, he says that resistance is provoked because the subject matter impinges on what many people consider to be "the fortress of personal privacy." Such persons regard feelings, values, and beliefs as inviolate and not open to study and discovery. They feel that "your behavior is your own business as long as you don't hurt others." What they overlook is that a disturbed child does hurt others. He/she is a burden on the teacher, a trial for peers, and a drain on the school system's resources. Later he/she may be the responsibility of society as a patient in a mental hospital, as a welfare recipient, or as a criminal, alcoholic, or drug addict. It is essential that we implement programs which can effectively contribute to the development of the psychological capabilities and competencies of children. If our research on the subject of human growth and development has taught us anything, it surely has taught us that children are in a state of growth and that skills, abilities, feelings, and attitudes are developmentally determined. Competent children have a balanced intelligence, an adequate fund of knowledge, sound personalities, and most important, competent children become competent adults.

Children's Needs

All educators know what children need. Unfortunately, no two educators agree on what these needs are! This paradox can be seen throughout the history of the organized school. It can be seen most clearly in contrasting the concepts of classical and progressive educational theory. Reducing these theories to rather simplistic and certainly primary terms, the proponents of the classical stance toward education believe that children need structure, organization, content, firm control and direction. The "progressives," under the influence of Rousseau and Dewey, lean toward exploration, discovery, self-direction, consequential experience, and expression.

Somewhere among and between these rather extreme positions we find every possible expression of educational organization and practice. Many of the systems so conceived and in use today borrow a bit from this, a little from that, and blend them into a conflicting hodgepodge with incompatible methods often leading to divergent and mutually exclusive goals. The purists and advocates of these various systems carry their ideas to the point that the means are obviously more important than the goal. Indeed, it seems sometimes that goals are not even established.

Probably the one thing that most educators could agree on is that their theories and methods should produce in the end a productive, useful, happy, and concerned citizen. The rub comes in defining what is meant by those terms and what the best methods and organizational structures are that will produce the desired outcome.

Personal Competency

What, for instance, is a productive person? What traits and characteristics does he or she have? Freud says that the healthy person is one who can work and love with satisfaction. Maslow (1954) calls the mentally healthy person self-actualized. His wide ranging description of such a person encompasses recognizing reality, an urge for self-improvement, accurate self-perceptions, creativity and spontaneity, a spirit of detachment and dignity, independence, capacity for ecstasy, and the ability to compassionately identify with one's fellows.

Jahoda's (1958) comprehensive study on the question of the attributes of good adjustment identified such qualities as one's attitude toward the self, the ability to realistically perceive the environment, and the capacity to mobilize one's resources to deal with life, as commonly agreed-upon qualities that signify good mental health in the individual. She felt that, as confused as concepts were about good mental health, the qualities that connote poor mental health were also in dispute. It appears that we don't know what a mentally healthy or disturbed person is really like. We know one when we see one though!

Relative and Absolute

Of course, we must not ignore the fact that good mental health, as such, is not an absolute. There are probably very few traits that are essential in every person and in all situations for the attainment of a satisfactory life adjustment. The situational factor is often ignored in attempts to describe the mentally healthy person. Surely the traits necessary to emotional stability in a prisoner-of-war camp are not the same as those that contribute to well-being for the business executive or school teacher.

In a prison, for instance, the ability to regress and isolate oneself emotionally and the capacity to fantasize and be self-sufficient are positively related to the maintenance of emotional stability. These same qualities may be restrictive or even handicaps to good life adjustment for the school teacher. In spite of the common sense fact that sound personalities can differ widely in their apparent characteristics, and regardless of the obvious relative effects of the life situation and its impact on the person, there are certain characteristics of well-adjusted, sound personalities that seem to be common to all people, cultures, and situations.

Dorothy Rogers (1957) provides us with a set of traits that seem to be found in most mentally healthy people, adults and children. She says that mentally healthy people feel positive about themselves. They see themselves as capable, adequate, and worthwhile. They don't describe themselves in derogatory terms and they don't need to belittle others to "bring them down to their size." Children who see themselves positively think that they can learn and that they are liked by teachers, their peers, and parents. They are challenged, not threatened, by new and difficult learning tasks. They regard failure or problems as temporary and surmountable and they don't feel "picked on" or singled out for punishment. Within developmental limitations, children who have a healthy self-concept can share and be helpful to other children. They are concerned about things and people in the world and not just in their own interests and activities. Such children, and adults, have more energy to spend in learning and living since they have to use very little of it to maintain a shaky personality structure (Rogers, 1951).

We could describe the person with a positive self-concept in much more detail. It is sufficient to note at this point that most people intuitively recognize such a person when they meet one. Mentally stable persons are comfortable and nonthreatening to be with. They have been called "health engendering" people. Children always respond actively and warmly to adults who have a secure sense of their own worth.

Dorothy Rogers goes on to say that the mentally healthy person establishes and maintains a satisfactory relationship to his/her environment. (S)He finds out what his responsibilities are and manages to meet societies' needs and his own by working out an acceptable reciprocal relationship.

(S)He deals effectively with life's problems. When frustrations and disappointments occur, he looks for ways to overcome or at least cope with them. The adequate person is struggling effectively with problems in his working life, social environment, and personal being rather than being overwhelmed or disorganized by stress and challenges.

Other characteristics that Rogers believes are common to mentally sound people include the ability to adapt to changing circumstances and the capacity to experience joy and pleasure. Such persons will establish and maintain, with any luck at all, an effective and satisfying way of life for themselves and their families.

How can children become healthy, fully-functioning adults? One important thing that every child should do is select healthy, stable, adjusted parents! Probably the most important variables that children have are the constitutional heredity and life experiences that they bring with them when they come to school. We have recognized that many attributes that contribute to life's success are products of a sound inheritance of good physical and personality traits and that the shaping effects of a secure, stable, benevolent early environment are vital to later adjustment and development. But second only in importance, in the developing life of every child, is the schooling experience. This experience can mean the difference in a life of success or one of tragedy for many, if not most children.

We can change a child's life. We can make substantial changes in his or her knowledge, skills, attitudes, values, feelings about him or herself and others, and in his or her capacity to cope effectively with life's vicissitudes and opportunities. One of the most direct ways we can change a child's life positively, to provide more options for controlling his/her future, is to teach the child experientially and substantively the "how" and "why" and "what" of human behavior. Good psychological adjustment can be taught and it can be learned by school children. As McCandless (1967) put it, "Objections to teaching human relations in schools are frequently expressed by some version of the cliché, 'the idea is fine, but you can't change human nature.' Research literature now includes enough studies (sociological and psychological, survey and experimental) to enable us to dismiss this generalization with confidence."

2

Teaching Behavioral Skills: Methods and Techniques

Skills and competencies in social and psychological behavior can be taught in the schools and can be learned effectively by children. In considering how this may be accomplished, we need to examine two related aspects of the task. First, the methods, organization, and techniques employed in the school setting may be utilized to enhance the behavioral competencies of the child. Second, content, materials, and learning experiences may be used to increase self-understanding and hence self-direction. These related perspectives of the goal of psychological competency are really not mutually exclusive. It is difficult to see how one would employ techniques and methods without, to some extent, being involved in the application of appropriate content and materials. Yet, it is possible to emphasize one more than the other.

The methodology emphasis stresses the experiences of the child in coping with the traditional content encountered in the school's curriculum. In this regard, methodology and techniques are secondary to the subject matter. One is still concerned primarily with the usual subject areas of reading, arithmetic, language arts, social studies, and science. However, the methodological emphasis shifts to techniques that enhance the child's efforts at mastery and lead him/her to see him/herself as capable and competent. His/her understanding of self and others becomes a by-product of an effective learning experience. From this perspective, the attitude of the teacher assumes a critical importance: the grading, grouping, and promotional practices of the school are vitally relevant; the ability and freedom of the child to explore, discover, and to go intellectually where his/her understandings lead are attributes of an effective school experience that culminate in a happy, productive, and well-adjusted student. Understanding and managing group interaction, cooperative interaction, and productive relationship skills are seen as ways to not only enhance the child as a learner in the traditional sense but also to develop psychological skills that can be used to foster further emotional and social growth.

On the other hand, a focus on materials and content plus specific attention to educational methodology are seen in efforts to teach psychological skills to children in a direct way. In this approach, exercises are designed that deal with certain affective processes, such as anger, resentment, and fear, which are important in the developing life of every child. Children are taught to understand the causes of human behavior; why people behave as they do, and how these feelings and beliefs affect their own action. Methodology is important as an effective learning experience, but it is secondary to the understanding and integration of those critical concepts by the child.

Methodology as a Focus

When we consider "what we do" as no more important than "how we do," we are stressing methods rather than content. From this vantage point, schools that stress the affective outcomes of the teaching process, as opposed to content knowledge, can be regarded as institutions with a concern for psychological education. However, such schools adopt the position that what children learn affectively is the outcome of how they are treated as individuals. In such schools, for instance, attempts are made to insure that grading practices are nonthreatening and that teachers encourage creativity and discovery. The curriculum is organized to accommodate the developmental level of the child and he/she is exposed to an atmosphere where subject mastery and achievement are always possible regardless of his/her maturity level or intellectual competency.

The most important comprehensive treatment of the philosophical position that *how* a school treats its children is more important than *what* it teaches them is contained in the report by the Bank Street College group. This effort, culminating in the book *The Psychological Impact of School Experience* (Biber, 1969), exemplifies the position that organization, techniques, methodology, and practice are the critical features in a psychologically sound program of education for children. Barbara Biber, in the preface to this study, cogently describes the perspectives and position of the proponents of this educational stance.

First, the quality of experience in school has a differential influence on all phases of development during the years of childhood. Knowledge of the interaction between cognitive and affective realms of functioning makes exclusive attention to intellectual skills an archaic and impractical goal for education. Instead, the competence of the child, which it is the school's responsibility to foster, must be broadly conceived in terms of ego strength, that is, the effective interaction of the individual with the work, the people, and the problems of his environment. This calls on the school to elevate its own competence to support simultaneously the growth of the cognitive functions represented in symbolizing, reasoning, problem solving and ordering information, and the personality processes related to feelings of self-worth and realization, potential for relating to people's autonomy and creativity, the capacity for emotional investment, and the building of a separate identity.

The further impact of the school experience in the life of the developing child, according to the Bank Street Group, was manifested by the effects of the internal processes in the child and his/her interaction in the classroom. The final tactical point that they make regarding the influence of the school may be the most important.

Finally, the promotion of positive mental health in a school cannot be treated as though it were an additional piece of subject matter, concerned with interpersonal relations, to be added to the curriculum. It involves, rather, the infusion of mental health principles into the educative process at all levels — to the way knowledge is transmitted as much as to the transmission of values implicit in the nature of the teacher-child relationship.

As we will see later, it is really not necessary to polarize this issue. It is possible to infuse a school with humanistic values, progressive teaching techniques, respect for the individual child, enhancement of discovery, exploration, and affective experiences and, at the same time, to add content to the curriculum which will greatly increase the probability that such goals will in fact be accomplished.

The task of the Bank Street group, in a nutshell, was to study the effects on children of two different educational philosophies and their attendant practices. These two approaches they called "Modern" and "Traditional." The Traditional school was characterized as aiming at intellectual growth and transmitting an established body of knowledge. It characterized teachers as final arbiters of right and wrong and stressed reliance on approved behavior, comparison and completion, and rewards and punishments as desirable ways to direct and enhance the educational experience of the child.

The Modern school, by contrast, relied on an appreciation of the dynamic forces in human behavior and on needs for socialization and respect for individual differences in children's needs and rates of growth. Authority is seen as relatively flexible and available for assumption by the children themselves as they mature. The goals of this educational approach include the intellectual growth of the child as well as the developed capacity to live and work with others and to ultimately function as a mature adult.

The outcomes of the study of the effects of the Modern versus Traditional schools are not really conclusive. There were certain clear differences in the self-concepts of children from the two different kinds of schools. Traditionally trained school children were more formally socialized and prestructured, while the Modern school group was seen as more open with differentiated images of themselves. The difference between the groups was even less clear as far as cognitive and interpersonal skills were concerned. One variable that did seem significant was the clear and unmistakable differential effects that schooling of both types had on boys in contrast with girls. It may be that a more cogent research question for the future is "What is the effect of personality structure and sex on the educational and psychological development of any given child."

The research outcomes of the Bank Street Study are really inconclusive. However, this report has given a clearer understanding of the forces, factors, and processes that blend to comprise the educational experience. Serious students concerned with affective education and the effects of the school environment on the personality development of the child should read the Bank Street Study as an essential primer on the subject.

Influencing the Interactional Processes in the School

The SEE Program

An interesting approach to influencing the affective development of the child has been pioneered by Norma Randolph (1966) in a process she calls Self Enhancing Education (SEE). The most interesting feature of this program is that it is essentially a teaching program in which the subject matter is "process." It is difficult at first to grasp the concept that we can teach and learn processes as well as content. In the Self Enhancing Education program, children are taught to use a process in their interaction in school experiences that will serve to enhance their effective functioning and hence their school achievement.

The thesis of this method is that behavioral problems, poor motivation, and unproductive achievement are caused by low self-esteem. The SEE program is designed to teach children to live and work more effectively thereby producing enhanced self-esteem. It is important to remember that this is a process learning task and not a substantive content learning task. The program consists of twelve specific processes which are approached both as individual learning tasks and as methods of facilitating school learning generally. These twelve processes, briefly summarized, are:

1. Problem solving
2. Self-management
3. Changing negative self-concept to positive
4. Building trust
5. Setting reasonable limits and attainable expectations
6. Freeing energy and directing it effectively
7. Stopping unproductive repetitive behavior
8. Assuming social responsibility
9. Developing physical abilities
10. Structuring success experiences
11. Promoting self-evaluation
12. Individualizing learning rates and tasks.

According to the authors (Randolph and Howe, 1966), these processes can be grouped around four major developmental clusters:

1. Those that help children feel stronger and more adequate about their academic competencies.
2. Those that help them feel physically more adequate.
3. Those that help them feel that they are unique resources of their own feelings in their interactions with significant adults.
4. Those that help them feel accepted by their peers as worthy individuals.

The authors of SEE believe that the development and modification of feelings and attitudes takes place primarily in the presence of oral-verbal interaction. Their training manual provides a detailed analysis of the procedures to be used in developing competencies in each of the twelve processes noted as the keys to the SEE program. One of the more detailed descriptions of one of these processes is that given for the initial teaching unit — the problem-solving process. A brief schematic summary of this unit is shown on pages 25, 26, and 27.

The SEE program is interesting and offers possibilities of real use in the school's efforts to teach children effective ways of behaving. It has the distinct advantage of being applicable to any subject matter. Furthermore, it can be taught to and learned by any age group in the school. The techniques of instruction are rather simple and could be easily learned by any teacher. Unfortunately, the training materials are somewhat difficult to understand and the wording is often vague and obscure in meaning. Most schools that use the SEE program have begun to do so after a training session conducted by one of the authors or by others who have had workshop training in the method.

The aim of the SEE program is to produce a child who can analyze concrete and abstract problems, who can make decisions, who can control him/herself, and who can relate effectively to others. There is little doubt that at least some of these goals can be accomplished through the processes learned in the program. However, it is difficult to understand how unconscious processes are revealed and examined and how any affective dimension, which has its own system of logic, can be forced into the logic of rationality. After all, much of human behavior is puzzling to the observer and to the experiencer precisely because it appears to be irrational. For all its apparent virtues, the SEE program seems to give little attention to this as one of the basic aspects of the human personality.

The Method of Transactional Analysis

Transactional Analysis (TA) is a method or program of developing sound emotional structure that relies very heavily on an understanding of dynamic and unconscious processes in human behavior.

TA is a process aimed at self-discovery and emotional growth. It incorporates a rather simple theory of personality structure and includes procedures for facilitating group interaction and self-management. The system is more completely and fully described by its developers and especially by Eric Berne in his books *Transactional Analysis in Psychoanalysis* (1961) and *Games People Play* (1964).

TA was first seen as a system of therapy for disturbed people. However, its simplicity, usefulness, high interest activities and

PROBLEM SOLVING*

Steps	Dialogue	Technique
1. State the problem as someone sees it — a child, a teacher, a principal, a parent. Symptomatic behaviors that lend themselves to problem solving: scapegoating, fighting, name calling (calling out after school to fight, etc.), using the lavatories as a playground, swearing, disrespectful comments.	"Our principal is concerned because there is so much name calling on the playgrounds." or "Johnny feels very hurt because he is being teased so much."	The teacher, or whoever presents Step 1, does so by investing the concern, problem, or need in the person who owns it. Example: "Our principal is concerned" . . . rather then . . . "There is too much name calling on the playgrounds," or, "You are name calling too much."
2. Gather significant data. Each person is encouraged to be the resource of his/her unique feelings and perception of the problem.	"I'm wondering if we can talk about what has been happening."	This is the time when the teacher has invited the children to talk about the problem. The teacher becomes the listener. However, he/she does this in a very active way by reflecting back feeling and content that are offered. Examples: "John, are you saying that it is painful to be left out of the game?" or "Sam, am I hearing you say that the name calling leads to fighting and calling out after school?"

*From Norma Randolph and William Howe, *Self Enhancing Education: A Program to Motivate Learners.* Palo Alto, California: Educational Development Corporation © 1966, pp. 26–28. Reprinted by permission of the publisher.

PROBLEM SOLVING (Cont.)

Steps

3. Clarify the hidden problem that the discussion reveals; ask for feedback concerning your classification. The clarification is often followed by other examples of the hidden problem and how it has been causing distress. Hidden problems that often emerge at Step 3: How to cope with differences. Often, how to cope with two varying value systems: the school's position, and the parent's advice. The hidden problem sometimes emerges as detachment or aloneness and an inability to make friends. A power struggle with adult-imposed rules. (Breaking the lavatory rules is so much fun it is worth the risk.) How to cope with authority figures who impose and control. How to cope with siblings who threaten the favored position with authority figures. A testing of limits about which there is doubt. How to cope with anger, or an expression of personal power. A conflict of cultural patterns. A need to gain peer status.

Dialogue

"From what you have been saying, I think maybe now I can put the pieces of this jigsaw puzzle together. You will have to tell me if they fit." (If no consensus, continue to gather data and clarify again).

Technique

If the teacher has listened perceptively to the data and has waited until all children who have something to offer have presented it, the data begins to emerge on a hidden problem. It may be that the children are trying to cope with differentness; or, are trying unsuccessfully to make friends. The hidden problem is what has been causing the symptomatic behavior such as fighting, calling names, and so on. At first, children usually cannot clarify the hidden problem. Once it is clarified, there is little doubt because of the children's reaction and the activation of many examples of their struggle with the problem.

4. Invite solutions.

"Now that we agree on our basic problem, what can we do about it?"

The teacher makes no judgemental statements of the solutions offered.

5. Summarize the solutions and agree to act on one or more alternatives.

"Is this, then, our favorite plan of action?"

The teacher grows skillful in summing up the solutions offered. Care should be taken not to differentiate out only the teacher's favorite solutions, but rather to sum up the gamut of alternatives offered. However, in case the solutions are all punitive, which they are sometimes (especially in the second grade), the teacher may, as a unique resource of his/her own feelings, express dissatisfaction with the punitive character of the offerings: "I don't like to be bossed and punished that much; I suspect you don't either. Can we think of any solutions that will allow each one to be more in charge of solving the problem?"

6. Provide for eventual evaluations.

"Suppose we try our plan for a week and then see how we feel and how we think it is working."

After the week of trial, the teacher again reviews the solution offered, asks for feedback about the efforts to solve the problem, and asks the students if they feel the solutions are working.

apparent effectiveness have caused proponents of the technique to extend TA to the development of sound personality structure through growth groups, encounter groups, management-development groups and teacher sensitivity workshops. It has been used in a variety of other settings where the goal was to improve the functioning of "normal" people rather than to repair the ravages of a distressed personality. Of course, TA is still in wide use in therapeutic settings also.

It seemed inevitable that someone would see the parallel between the growth needs of children and the developmental needs of immature adults and adopt TA for use in the schools with children. This is what Alvyn M. Freed (1971) has done in his brief manual *Transactional Analysis for Kids and Grown-Ups Too*. Dr. Freed says his TA manual was intended for children in grades three through six, although with modification it may be used also with other age groups. He has also recently published *TA for Tots* which is aimed at the pre-school to approximately nine-year-old child.

The tripartite personality structure of psychoanalysis is well known by most people today. Everyone has heard of Freud's id, ego, and superego. Unfortunately, hardly anybody really understands the concepts and complex processes included in these terms. The TA-presented personality structure on the other hand is much easier to comprehend. Our personalities, according to TA, are also made up of three parts: the *Parent,* the *Child,* and the *Adult.*

The Parent would correspond in a gross way to the superego of psychoanalysis. Our Parent is bossy, remembers rules and duties, punishes us when we misbehave, and is paradoxically both nurturing and kind, autocractic and punitive. The Parent in us wants to be helpful and sympathetic but also enforces rules and regulations. It is the Parent talking when we say, "Sit down, you must be tired. Let me get you a hot drink." But it is also our Parent speaking when we say, "Son, you broke the lamp, you are a careless, unthinking boy!" Whether the Parent in us, according to TA theory, is basically kind and nurturing, or authoritative and hostile depends on the message we incorporate from our real parents in our own childhood.

The second aspect of the personality, according to TA theory, is the Child. The Child is apparently the reservoir of affectivity. Pleasure, joy, sadness, fear, anger, and resentment are all products of the Child in our personalities. It is the Child in us that has fun, acts uninhibitedly, or frets immaturely. It is the Child that says, "I feel great today for some reason," or conversely, "They don't like me because they didn't invite me to their party." Freed calls the

Child the most important aspect of our personalities. In analytic terms we can equate TA's Child to Freud's id.

Adult, in TA, is roughly comparable to the ego concept of psychoanalytic theory. It is the Adult that acts on the basis of reality, who works, makes decisions, and carries out the business of living. The Adult is what we think with. It is the Adult that says, "Well let's see. I believe that this part fits here."

In the Freed program, children learn to recognize, in their own behavior and interaction with others, what motivates them and what the consequences and causes of their behavior really are. Children are taught to ask themselves, "What am I saying?" "How are others acting toward me?" This kind of analysis will tell the child what aspects of his personality are controlling his behavior.

There are other key concepts in the TA system. *Strokes,* for instance, are important as reinforcers of behavior. Strokes may be as concrete as candy to eat or as abstract as a smile or kind word. The older the child, the more likely the strokes will take the form of social reinforcers.

Stamps in the TA system represent the hoarding of rebuffs, fears, and resentments. People save "brown" stamps and when they have enough they feel justified to express anger, hostility, and to act unfairly toward others. Some people are avid and chronic collectors of brown stamps! Many underachieving children, according to Freed, are always alert to the possibility of adding to their collection of brown stamps.

The TA system describes games we play that are contrary to good emotional development and suggests ways we can stop engaging in such self-destructive behavior. It also includes descriptions of ways to develop mature, responsible behavior through activities that are involved in *promises, agreements,* and *contracts,* other key TA concepts.

The program described in Freed's manual includes chapters on each of the key concepts in TA theory which can be read by or to children. A part of the chapter on "Strokes" is reprinted as a sample of the kinds of material in this program.

STROKES*

Have you noticed how cats and dogs like to be petted, stroked, fed, played with and talked to? You and I are the same way. When we were little we were petted, touched, talked to and played with by Mom and

* From Alvyn M. Freed, *Transactional Analysis for Kids and Grown-ups, Too.* Sacramento, California: Jalmar Press, Inc. © 1971, pp. 32, 34, 36. Reprinted by permission of the publisher and author.

Dad and these actions felt good. They pleased me. I call those actions which give me those pleasant feelings "strokes". A hand on my shoulder is a stroke. A hug is a stroke. "Hello!" is a stroke. Sometimes someone does something to me which is unpleasant, like a slap. That can be a stroke, too. An unpleasant stroke. But all strokes stir you up. If you don't get them you'll get sick. Strokes are like food. We must have them and once we get them we will do anything for more of them.

A friend of mine calls strokes that feel good "warm fuzzies." [1] He calls strokes that hurt "cold pricklies." Sometimes when we think we can't get a warm fuzzie we will work to get a cold prickly. Any stroke is better than no stroke. Do you ever work to get a cold prickly? (To get a spanking.) One time doctors and nurses in a big hospital discovered that babies that were not being stroked because nobody lifted or cuddled them or cooed over them got sick. They seemed to give-up wanting to live, and some stopped living. At the same time the doctor discovered that the babies who were cuddled and stroked, grew strong and healthy. From that time on the doctor told the nurses to stroke the babies. All the babies were stroked and nobody got sick. [2]

Do you like strokes? I do — what's your favorite "warm fuzzie"? How do you like to be stroked — a back rub, smile, an "A" or what? Talk about it to your mother today. Talk about it now.

When we're little babies we need to be touched often. Touching makes us go. We've already learned that if babies don't get strokes they may get sick and die. We never stop needing strokes. Later we learn to like smiles, kind looks and words (like "good"). They're strokes, too! A friend of mine says stroking is best when it's for being. Most often parents give us strokes for doing. Later we'll learn what happens when we think we can't do what others expect of us.

If I don't get strokes, I feel bad. When I get strokes I feel good. Any stroke is better than no stroke. Strokes from spanking, yelling, name calling and bossing are cold pricklies but they are better than no strokes. "Cold pricklies" are better than no "warm fuzzies". Sometimes when I think nobody loves me (will give me strokes) I try to make them mad — at least I'll get them to know I'm there and they'll stroke me (even though it hurts).

The strokes that I like best are friendly words, my own name, somebody to touch me, rub my back, hug me and even kiss me (if not too often or too sloppy). How do you get strokes? What kind do you like?

To have very few strokes or no strokes at all is like not living. Some strokes are given to me because people like me. These I get free. When I don't get strokes for free, I do things to get strokes. Like I will

[1] Reference: Steiner, Claude M., Ph.D., Transactional Analysis Bulletin, Volume 9, No. 36, October, 1970.

[2] Reference: Berne, Eric, M.C., *Games People Play,* © 1964, Grove-Press.

help someone and they will thank me. "Thank you," is an earned stroke. Sometimes I will bug mother or sister until they yell at me or hit me. These things hurt but they are strokes. Other times I will be a good boy and they will tell me that I am good. What I need most are the free strokes, just for being me.

In this chapter you have learned about strokes, good strokes, hurt strokes, earned strokes and free strokes. How do you get strokes? Talk about this. What kind do you get most? From whom? Who do you like getting strokes from? How come? What do you do to get them? Is this the best way?

1. What is a stroke?
2. Why do we need strokes?
3. What kinds of strokes are there?
4. What is a free stroke?
5. Tell how to earn strokes.
6. Give somebody in the group a free stroke.
7. Are all strokes pleasant?

Transactional Analysis as a growth tool for the developing child seems to be a promising system. It is organized, systematic, and has precise goals. These traits are especially desirable in programs that would become a part of the school curriculum. Obviously, such a program would have to be established, at least initially, as a separate content area. Until children learned the concepts and procedures and until they had progressed far enough in their own understanding and development, TA could not be readily incorporated into other content areas. However, it is easy to see that it could be incorporated into virtually every phase of activity in the elementary school after preliminary training and experience with the system. As a method of increasing self-awareness and understanding, it certainly deserves consideration by any educators concerned about the affective growth of their students.

However, TA lends itself to superficiality because of one of its principle virtues, simplicity. For this reason, devotees of the system are often guilty of glibly labeling behavior and gleefully spotting other persons' hangups and problems without recognizing their own difficulties. TA can be misused to restrict growth and retard openness and freedom. The system unfortunately has been on occasion misused by ill-trained and dubiously motivated persons, although this is true to some degree for any method or theory and practice. Teachers should have preliminary training and experience with TA before they try to incorporate the techniques in their classrooms. There are a number of reputable pupil personnel workers and other educators all over the country who have sound professional backgrounds and special training in TA who can work with teachers and administrators in incorporating TA techniques and understanding in their educational practices.

Children and Behavioral Sciences

Sheldon Roen (1967) organized a behavioral sciences teaching program which he taught a fourth-grade group in Hingham, Massachusetts in 1963–64. His classroom exercises were organized around group discussions in which questions like "How are people different?" and "What are people like?" served as a springboard to a deeper look at people's motivation and behavior. Maturation and child development were considered along with stages of development and appropriate age-related behaviors. The importance and influence of such psychological factors as inheritance and environment were studied, relating these concepts to motives and feelings. More traditional topics such as learning and perception were also covered. Among other general areas that were included were:

1. self-identity
2. social factors
3. research concepts
4. anthropology
5. emotions

Roen suggests that such content be offered to every elementary child in the interest of preventative mental health and with a view toward the subsequent development of interest in children in the behavioral sciences as a field of study. He believes that such teachers should be trained as behavioral science specialists, preferably at the master's degree level, to offer children classes in psychology once or twice a week as a regular subject in the school's curriculum.

Roen (1967) goes on to say that, "Those who are able to see the school's role as extending beyond the teaching of the three R's should not find it difficult to justify the behavioral sciences as being important enough to be included in the elementary school curriculum — especially if they consider the progress made by proponents of foreign languages and the physical sciences."

Schell (1967) agrees with Roen's strategy and proposes a curriculum for training teachers of psychology for the elementary and high school. He would approach this problem by adding to the skills of school psychologists, elementary school counselors, and regular teachers. He suggests restructuring the training of the school psychologist to better prepare this specialist (especially at the high school level) to offer a psychologically based course to high school students. He would add an additional year of intensive training to the counselors' program to enable this worker to add teaching and curriculum consultation in the behavioral sciences to his/her repertoire of skills. Finally, he suggests offering a minor in teaching psychology to the certification for elementary teachers, feeling that this may represent the largest untapped pool of available expertise.

The entire Spring, 1967 issue of the *Journal of School Psychology* (Volume 5) containing articles by Roen, Schell and others, is devoted to the topic "Teaching Psychology and the Behavioral Sciences in the Schools." Anyone seriously interested in this subject would do well to study these articles for background, ideas, and further reference.

Home-School-Community

One interesting approach to the use of behavioral instruction as a way to strengthen the psychological resources of school children was the project entitled *Home-School-Community Systems for Child Development*, undertaken in the Atlanta City Schools with the support of an NIMH grant. This project, which was in operation from July 1970 to August 1973, showed promise as an organizational effort to bring relevant resources to bear on the emotional growth of the developing child.

The project's primary goal was to develop and demonstrate the application of a curriculum based on behavioral science principles, appropriate for kindergarten through fourth grade, which could be offered by regular classroom teachers without extensive preparation. Its general goal was to prevent the development of later emotional and social problems in children.

This project incorporated the concepts, discussed in this monograph, of Ojemann, Randolph, Long, and many others, adapted for use in the schools by teachers and in the community with the child's parents. This multifaceted approach to the problems of "affective education," as it was termed, was apparently very successful, based on the evaluation of the short-term effects on children, teachers, and parents. The long-term influence of the program should be studied since a wealth of research data carefully collected and described is available, seldom the case in such programs.

The evaluation of the research data led the investigators to conclude that the Home-School-Community program:

1. provided positive changes in social casualty concepts
2. improved classroom social behavior

3. had limited effect on male students
4. was especially effective with low socio-economic students
5. demonstrated the need to involve parents in any program designed to teach behavioral principles to children.

The summary report on this project, *Home-School-Community Systems for Child Development: A Final Progress Report* (August 31, 1973, NIMH Grant #ROI MH 16666-01AZ), is an excellent primer and review of the general field of affective education for children. In addition to a description of the organization and operation of the project itself, one can find a review of the available literature on the subject as well as instructional programs, packages and material, media kits, filmstrips, books, professional literature, and program units. It includes a discussion of the rationale, purposes, and outcomes of a program of affective education. A complete curriculum guide along with detailed lesson plans are included in the report.

The scope of the program was wide, but the sequence of objectives was logically based and the program grew out of the stated goals of the investigators. As it was summarized by the project staff, the purposes of the Home-School-Community operation were:

1. to develop a curriculum based on concepts from behavioral science disciplines to be taught to children in kindergarten through fourth grade.
2. to develop a curriculum to present these concepts to parents which would help them to support and extend the in-school activities.
3. to develop a training program for teachers which would prepare them to teach the behavioral sciences curriculum; and
4. to implement the H-S-C program in the classroom, through a program of parent education and through cooperation with community resources.

Behavioral Sciences Applied

Barbara Ellis Long (1970) has written a clear and concise description of her efforts to develop a curriculum and accompanying methodology to teach behavioral principles to elementary children.

With an eye toward preventing emotional disturbance in children, she began a series of weekly sessions with a sixth-grade group from Webster College Experimental Schools in St. Louis. Later, fourth and fifth graders were added.

Long employed the discovery method of teaching as described by Bruner (1963). The typical 30-minute periods were nondirective games and experiments. The most successful periods were spent in active participation. One of the keys to an effective program in this area is activity. As Long says:

This subject cannot be taught to children effectively by lecture and assigned readings. The children simply have to try it. They are not mature enough to absorb general discussions and descriptions alone. For them, the abstract must come after the specific experience.

Among the topics covered in the course of the program were perception, learning, emotions, child development, and personality. Role playing and simulation games were widely employed. Although no formal validation of the program was attempted, the children were reported to have made obvious gains in understanding behavior and in developing a causal approach to the problem of living. The children enjoyed the work and reported to the class willingly and happily. The program was introduced into the St. Louis public schools in collaboration with the Southwest St. Louis Community Mental Health Center.

A series of lessons on human relations prepared by Long and her colleagues has appeared in the journal *Grade Teacher* (April, 1972). These lessons are models of ways to approach sensitive, complex behavioral principles in simple, understandable ways.

These materials have been collected, updated, and organized into a middle school psychology curriculum. This unit includes a guide for the teacher, a cassette, a set of slides, and activity sheets for students. Reprinted here is a section of one lesson from chapter 9 of the teacher's manual, *The Journey to Myself*.

Chapter IX: The Search for Meaning*

A. *"Why do people do what they do?"*

This lesson is really a model for any number of lessons — a format for helping the children develop good questions which they might proceed to answer for themselves by their own joint discussions and their own investigations.

The children form small groups to make up their own questions about "Why do people do what they do?" Each small group chooses one question for full class discussion.

Some very good things can develop from these open discussions. They are often just the right element to loosen up a dull time of the year. They give you, the teacher, some ideas on where to go next, and generally convince the students that it is their classroom, after all.

This format is useful for conducting discussions with all kinds of groups of any age level. It is, in some respects, another kind of brainstorming, but one which can lead to a great degree of specificity, if you choose.

I began using this model with the children in the first pilot study

---

* From Barbara Ellis Long, *The Journey to Myself*. Austin, Texas: Steck-Vaughn Co. (forthcoming). Reprinted by permission of the publisher.

class that I conducted in 1967–68 at Webster College School in St. Louis. I have since used it many times and in many places. That time, I was developing curriculum, and had reached the point of pure panic because I was completely blank about what to cook up for the next lesson. So, I simply asked the children to invent some questions about "Why do people do what they do?"

I suspected they'd have a few ideas for me, and I was not wrong. I now have files full of questions that students have dreamed up, and pages of notes about their discussions. These are my most prized research data. They're also a record of some of my happiest moments.

These open-discussion times based on the children's questions can also be answers to problems other than just "What do we do next?" When things are getting dull, when something is going on in the classroom that needs ventilation and you just can't come flat out with it, when you want an idea of what they've gotten out of the class so far, when you feel everybody needs to have a little fun . . . that's when you try this.

This format is also very useful near the end of the school year, when the children are becoming restless, and you, the teacher, are reaching the end of your tether too. It is an indirect way of saying that ideas that begin at school do have some relationship to ideas outside of school. The implication is there that if Summer comes, can Fall and growing up be far behind? You're implicity suggesting that they — the students — are indeed growing up. Their ideas are valuable, and their investigations can be important too. That's a nice note on which to finish the school year.

This kind of open-ended, question-inventing activity is really an arrangement whereby the children are encouraged to test out their own ideas with their peers, and to practice the abstract verbal analysis of problems. They can then be supported while they develop further hypotheses or questions which they can proceed to check out by their own efforts, if they wish. That takes them full circle: from creative verbal play to abstractions, to some pragmatic testing, and back again to abstract analysis of results and further creative thinking. At these middle school ages, that spiraling process is often very active and can be encouraged easily to open up greater possibilities for creative growth and development.

Human behavior is a good subject on which to hang this kind of problem-solving activity, because everybody has had experience with it. In addition, the urge to *know* is already built in. The teacher is not in the position of having to convince the students that the subject is worth studying. The children also have the chance to validate some ideas about a number of things which are important to them within the school setting.

Incidentally, there is absolutely no substitute for the notes you make right after something like this, even if they are all misspelled and written on a napkin. You will bless yourself, months later. Video tape and sound recordings are also as precious as gold, for many purposes. Insights that leap out of these records so strikingly, after the course is over are often more valuable than any test results, because the *process* comes clear as well as the results.

PROCEDURE:
Time required: One to four class periods. This could go on indefinitely, but sooner or later, most youngsters will want concrete action, and the less verbal children will become tired of "all that talk."
Materials needed: Pencils and laboratory manuals, (page ____) plus the chalkboard. (Also, perhaps, a joint need to get off the usual classroom merry-go-round and just "talk.")

Ask the children to form small groups of four to six members each. Each group elects a secretary. Then simply tell them:

"*Think up some questions about why people do what they do.*"
"Huh? What do you mean?" etc. Explain to them.

"*You've probably always wondered about all sorts of funny things that you see people do. Now is your chance to try to figure out some of those things together. Maybe we can find some answers, or some ways to find out the answers. You can ask any kind of question you like about why people do what they do. Get your group secretary to write them down. Each secretary write down his or her group's questions in the laboratory manual, page ____.*"

Try not to give examples, but if you are hard pressed, and there is lots of open-mouthed panic, try:

"*Here are a few questions some other children have asked:*
'*Why do people get mad when you show them they are wrong about something?*'
'*Why do people cry over spilled milk?*'
'*Why don't boys wash as much as girls do?*'
'*Why do we have tests?*'
'*Why do you feel as if you're going to cry sometimes, even when you don't want to?*' "

Choose what you like from these, or invent something you'd like to talk about yourself. Anything goes.

After they get started, they can go on like this for hours. When each group has decided on five or six questions, call a halt.
Tell them:

"*OK, now choose one question on your group list that is the one your group wants to talk about with the class. Secretaries; mark the question your group chooses with a star on page ____.*"

You can bet they have already been talking about their questions. The room is probably already pretty noisy. That's one thing about children and ideas — they do get noisy. This kind of oral problem solving does generate racket. So, shut the door if you can.

Once they have done their choosing — not without a certain amount of squabbling, no doubt — write all the questions on the chalkboard.

Take a vote on which question the class wants to talk about first, second, third, . . . , or choose the one *you* want to lead off with. Don't underestimate your own hunch about the best way to begin.

Discussion: Your main job during these discussions is just to make sure that the children do the talking, and that the talk keeps on going. Anything you can do to keep it going is to the good. Remember: you can't shape behavior if there is no behavior to shape. The main thing here is to have lots of conversation going.

If you see your own role as that of referee and devil's advocate, you'll do very well. You are actually aiming at promoting arguments or debates, and making the children prove their points.

Discussion depends upon talk — and there can therefore be no discussion if there is no talk. And not just any talk. You will need more than just noise. Your job is to keep your eyes and ears open for something that takes things farther on down the line toward any answer, any idea, any lead for *further* analysis.

Many ideas and suggestions on teaching the behavioral sciences can be found in the quarterly magazine *People Watching: Curriculum and Techniques for Teaching the Behavioral Sciences* (1971) as well as in Long's new book, *Ideas for People Watchers* published by Herder and Herder. There are many exciting and interesting features of the programs and lessons contained in the "People Watchers" curriculum. However, one of the major drawbacks to the program is that teachers who use it must be well-trained, sensitive, and oriented toward the behavioral sciences as a legitimate field of academic and experiential learning. Teachers would have to receive more training in behavioral management, counseling and relationship skills than they do now if the program were to become an integral part of the elementary school curriculum. Appropriately trained school counselors and school psychologists may very well provide the instructional leadership and consultation necessary to the effective employment of this program.

Guidance Learnings

A most interesting approach to the task of teaching children to understand and use psychological concepts in their own lives was developed by the staff of PROJECT DIRECT, a Title III, Elementary and Secondary Education Act project in Georgia (undated). This project was designed to offer remedial and developmental psychological services to all kindergarten through third grade children in four rural school systems.

One phase of the program concerned the offering of clinical services to schools and children in the form of psychological evaluation, diagnosis, and consultation. In a sense, this group of services could be called the remedial or treatment phase of the program. The other major thrust of the program was developmental in nature and oriented toward psychological processes. It involved structured exercises planned for children and carried out in the classroom setting. These exercises were designed to help children develop effective and enhancing ways of seeing themselves and of relating to others. The developmental objectives outlined by the authors of the exercises, Barbara Jackson and Don Lott, were concerned with two major themes: (1) Development of the Self Concept, and (2) Development of Inter-Personal Relationship Skills. The "lessons" prepared to teach these concepts were called *Guidance Learnings*.

The topics which were covered by the exercises that related to development of a sound self concept included (1) awareness of the self, the environment of feelings, and the development of appropriate ideas of one's abilities and limitations; (2) understanding and acceptance of one's self, of others, of social roles, of imagination and expression, of choices and decisions, of problem solving; and (3) developing norms and personal values.

The second major developmental objective, enhancement and refinement of interpersonal relationships, covered such topics as (1) interpersonal communications, including self-expression and listening; (2) understanding relationships, including sensitivity to others, freedom from prejudice, dependent and cooperative needs, frustration and anger; and (3) learning the value of mutuality in relationships, including the role of authority, group efforts and the reciprocity of feelings expressed and received.

To teach these concepts, staff members of the project went into classrooms and demonstrated one of the *Guidance Learnings* with children in the classroom. Subsequently teachers were expected to be able to follow the appropriate lesson plans in teaching future topics.

These learnings plans were developed for all four grade levels although some of the lessons could be utilized at more than one grade level. A total of twenty-three exercises were developed for use in the kindergarten; thirty-one for the first grade; thirty for the second grade; and thirty-two for use at the third grade level. A sampling of the titles of the exercises includes "Who are You?", "Having a Friend", "How Do You Feel?", "Chatterbox", "Sometimes People Are Good", and the "Left Out Game." Each exercise is prefaced with a brief description of the focus of the activity, the objectives, and methods and materials needed to teach that particular lesson.

With permission of the copyright holder, The Georgia Department of Education, one of the exercises is reprinted below to give a flavor of the kinds of materials that were developed and used.

Guidance Learning
"Games for the Five Senses"

1. *FOCUS:* Development of self-concept.
2. *OBJECTIVE:* Awareness of the senses and the importance of utilizing them to the field of experiences.
3. *METHOD:*
   A. Personnel involved: Counselor, PPA, Teacher
   B. Procedure: Have all materials in a large paper bag hidden from pupils' view.

   Introduction: "Boys and Girls, We are going to play some games. To have the most fun, it is necessary for everyone to follow instructions carefully. For the first game, I will show you what to do and then tell you when to do it. First, watch me but wait to do it when I tell you." (The leader demonstrates by closing his eyes and covering his ears.)

   "Now everyone do what I just did; close your eyes tightly and cork your ears."

   (Spray room with pine-scented spray. Obtain the children's attention by clapping loudly and asking them to open their eyes.)

   "Do you notice something? What could it be?" When they recognize the scent, ask: "How did you know? Can you feel it? Can you see it?"

   Tell the children that there are four other ways of knowing what is happening around them and see if they can name them (seeing — hearing — touching — tasting). Tell them you would like to play some games with them to show them some ways of knowing.

   TOUCH GAME: Select 4 volunteers to come to the front of the room and blindfold them. Take the bag with object for "Touch Game" and let each person feel what is in the bag but not to tell what they feel until asked. After all volunteers have a turn, ask each one what he felt in the bag. Then take out all objects for the class to see. Ask the volunteers if it was difficult to tell what the objects were without seeing them.

   SMELL GAME: Select four other volunteers and blindfold them. Tell them to smell the objects you hold under their noses but do not tell what it is until asked. Allow all four to smell first object and ask each one to identify it. Repeat with all objects for "Smell Game."

TASTE GAME: Select 2 more volunteers and blindfold them. Tell them to hold their noses so they can't smell anything and with toothpicks place a small piece of apple in one child's mouth and a small piece of potato in the second child's mouth. Have them tell what they are tasting while still holding their noses. Without the sense of smell it will be difficult to tell one from the other.

SIGHT GAME: Ask the children to close their eyes as if they were blind. Write on the chalkboard a word or sentence. "What happened? What would it feel like not to be able to see? Would you miss very much?"

In conclusion, remind the children that they could not have participated in the activity without using the sense of hearing. Could they learn from their teacher if they could not hear?

C. *Interpretation:* This activity emphasizes to the children the importance of being aware to experiences through all five senses. Without the senses one could not learn, for they are the gateway to our world of experiences.

4. *MATERIALS:*
   1. Four men's handkerchiefs.
   2. Pine-scented spray.
   3. Touch game: brown bag, yarn, nail, rubber band, sandpaper, play-doh.
   4. Smell game: lemon, scented talc powder, ground coffee, newspaper, bar of soap.
   5. Taste: apple, potato.
   6. Toothpicks and instrument to slice apple and potato.
5. *SUGGESTED FOLLOW-UP FOR TEACHERS:* The following discussion questions might be explored:
   1. What could happen on the play-ground if you could not see? If you could not feel?
   2. Could you describe a tree or a flower if you had never been able to see?
   3. What would it be like watching T. V. if you could not hear?
6. *EVALUATION:*
   Note:
   1. Children's reactions.
   2. Appropriateness for age group and grade level.
   3. Conciseness and clarity of instruction.

The major advantages of a program such as this are the clear, concise lesson plans, the high interest such material has for children, and the specific focus of the exercise on a determined developmental task. Also, a minimum of special preparation or training is required by teachers who are to use the program.

The learnings activities however, require that time be set aside for this purpose. For this reason, some teachers with a determined attitude toward academic "relevance" for all school material, fail to use the materials with necessary attention and enthusiasm. In addition, more learning exercises need to be developed to cover adequately all the developmental concepts identified as essential to sound emotional growth.

Research on the outcome of the program was generally positive. In fact, academically oriented teachers would be surprised to learn that the "treated" group showed substantially better academic gains than did the control group of children. Social gains were demonstrated for children exposed to the program as were smaller, but positive, gains in emotional adjustment. One positive outcome of the program was the confirmed observation that teachers were more flexible and open in their attitudes toward their children after experience with the program and they were more knowledgeable about principles of child development.

3

Teaching Behavioral Skills:
Curriculum and Program

Causal Approach to Human Behavior

Ralph H. Ojemann and his associates (1972) have pioneered in the development of programs, processes and materials designed to teach fundamental principles of human behavior to elementary children. These efforts have culminated in a series of handbooks entitled, *A Teaching Program in Human Behavior and Mental Health: Handbook for Teachers*. Handbooks are available for the first through the fifth grades.

Ojemann (1972) holds that the schools do a relatively good job of teaching children about their physical environment but that little time and attention is devoted to helping the child understand and cope with his/her social-emotional world. He contends that children learn to comprehend behavior in simplistic, superficial terms and that attention needs to be devoted to teaching children ways to perceive and appreciate that people do things in response to their environment and that they feel because of the behavior of others and how it affects them. He asserts that one of the major tasks confronting schools is in designing a curriculum and using instructional techniques that teach children how to comprehend the dynamics of human behavior. He terms this teaching process a *causal approach* to understanding behavior. The basic manual describing the program and providing a rationale for its use is titled, *Developing a Program for Education in Human Behavior* (1972), and is available from the Educational Research Council of America, The Rockefeller Building, 614 Superior Avenue (W), Cleveland, Ohio 44113.

According to Ojemann, children who are taught to appreciate human behavior in the causal sense grow in their ability to manage and control their own behavior in constructive, productive ways. They gain the ability to recognize the complexities of behavior and to realize that all available information should be gathered and considered before decisions are made. They begin to consider alternative ways of responding to situations and to ponder the outcomes of various alternatives. Children see teachers as helpers and as guides rather than as punitive authority figures and they learn to seek and use help more effectively. Children trained in the causal approach to human behavior take responsibility for working out problems constructively, and they begin to see their problems as potentially approachable and solvable. They can introspect and see in themselves how they feel and think in stressful and unpleasant situations. Such children are able to appreciate their parents and realize that everyone has basic needs and feelings, including the people who care for and guide them. Finally, as they learn more about others and why they behave and feel as they do, they are able to work, play, and relate to others in constructive, healthful ways.

The materials and programs of the causal behavior series are unique in several ways, not the least of which is the combination of methods and organized instructional materials. Causal methods are described which are applicable to teaching behavioral understanding in any subject matter area, including science and arithmetic, as well as in reading, language arts, and social studies. At the same time, narrative units have been developed which focus on specific behavioral outcomes and which are designed for use by the teacher. So, in this program, we have a full spectrum of organization from theory to process, to structure, to technique and methods. In addition, the very pertinent observation is made that causal thinking as a process can be introduced in the natural setting of the school and in its everyday activities. Children can learn causal behavior by observing how and what their teachers do. They can learn causal orientation through meaningful content in any subject matter discipline, and finally they can participate in causal approaches to problem solving in contemporary classroom and playground activities.

With permission of the publisher, we will reproduce one of the narratives developed for use by the classroom teacher. The story is from the handbook for the first grade and is a beginning step in attempting to teach children that behavior is caused; that people do things for some reason or reasons. This story-activity is entitled "The Broken Crayon."

THE BROKEN CRAYON*

To the Teacher

It isn't helpful to look at the behavior and then make a snap judgment as to what happened and what should be done about it. Behind every form of behavior are causes. Not until we find the causes, will we be able to decide what might be done.

Suggestions for Using the Story

This story is a good one to use to let the children supply their own endings for the story. The teacher might introduce the story by saying:

"Today we have a story about a group of boys and girls who were angry with each other. I want you to try to think about why they were angry and how this problem might have come about. After I've read part of the story, I'm going to stop and see if you can tell me how you think the story might end."

Several possible breaking-off points are suggested below. The teacher can decide which breaking-off point best suits the maturity and creativity of her group.

1. When Miss Gray asks herself: "How could it have happened without anyone knowing it? Why will no one say it is his crayon? What can be done to make the children friends again?"

These questions indicate a causal approach on her part, but as yet no indication of reasons are given.

2. After reading: "Miss Gray thought of several plans that would help the children to be glad to work together again."

Here the teacher might ask, "Now what do you suppose those plans might be?" Again no direct indication of a causal approach is given although Miss Gray has thought of several non-causal ways of handling the problem.

3. After Nancy said: "Oh dear! I can't find my red crayon." This gives the first clue as to what might have happened and would make it easier for the children to finish the story.

4. After Miss Gray said: "No, don't look at your neighbor. Everyone look at the soles of your own shoes."

Here a rather direct indication of the cause is given and the children should be able to bring the story to an appropriate ending.

---

* From Ralph H. Ojemann, *Education in Human Behavior: Handbook for First-Grade Teachers*. Cleveland: Educational Research Council of America, © 1961, pp. 33–36. Reprinted by permission of the publisher.

The Broken Crayon

"Look, Miss Gray! Someone smashed his crayon on the floor — just after we got our room all cleaned up!" said Jim.

Since this was the day the mothers were coming to see the puppet show, all the children had helped to make the classroom nice and neat. Some of the children had dusted, some had straightened up the reading table, and some of the boys had even given up most of their noon hour to scrub the floor. All the children were careful to wipe their feet before coming into the room.

The bell had just rung and Jim was the last one to his seat. As he took his seat, he noticed the crayon on the floor, right where one could see it from the door. Not just a crayon that could be picked up either, but one that had been crushed and smeared in a big, ugly red blotch across the clean floor.

Jim looked at it, Miss Gray looked at it, and the rest of the children looked at it. They got out of their seats and stood around all talking at once.

"Who do you suppose did it, Miss Gray? Whoever did shouldn't be allowed to see our show this afternoon," said Bill.

"Bet I know who did it," said Jerry. Several of the children thought they knew who had done it, but they were not sure. They began to blame each other.

"What are you going to do to the one who did it, Miss Gray?" asked Jean.

For a minute, Miss Gray thought someone should be punished, too. She thought, just as the children did, that someone should be willing to tell that he stepped on the crayon — but no one did.

No one wanted to clean up the crayon, and surely no one was feeling very happy.

"They're not really angry with each other. They are only disappointed because this has spoiled their clean floor after all the hard work," thought Miss Gray.

When she thought about this, she did not want to scold anyone. She was sorry, too, and went to the closet to get the brush and dust pan.

"I'll clean it up, Miss Gray," offered Dick when he saw her with the brush.

"I'll help, too," said Bill.

In a minute the boys had fixed things up as good as new again, but this did not keep the children from being cross with each other.

"I have a pretty good idea who did it," Dick whispered to Bill. "And I'm going to find out for sure after school."

All this time, Miss Gray was thinking very hard about the crushed crayon. How could it have happened without anyone knowing it? Why will no one say it is his crayon? What can be done to make the children friends again?

She then remembered when one of her teachers, several years before, had kept the whole class after school until someone said he had broken a rule. Miss Gray had never been sure that that boy had not simply said it was his fault so that they could all go home.

(Do you think it would help if Miss Gray would keep these boys and girls after school to find out who stepped on the crayon?)

Miss Gray did not think it had seemed a very good way to learn what had happened. She did not want these children to feel as she had felt at that time.

It could have been carelessness, but the children were not apt to be careless when they had worked so hard to have things looking nice. After all, it was not so serious that a crayon had been crushed, but it was serious that the children were angry with one another, and that they did not trust each other.

"Maybe some child is afraid and that is why he doesn't tell," thought Miss Gray. "Or, perhaps it was just an accident. Maybe no one knows who did it."

Miss Gray thought of several plans that would help the children to be glad to work together again.

"Boys and girls, how would you like to draw a border for our room? We have a little time before the bell rings, and I'm sure your mothers would like it very much."

The children were delighted and soon were drawing as busy as bees.

"Oh, dear! I can't find my red crayon," said Nancy.

"Maybe it was yours that fell on the floor," answered Peter.

"But, I haven't even had my box of crayons out of my desk until now," said Nancy quickly.

Suddenly Carol remembered that she had borrowed Nancy's crayon during the last art period. She had not returned it until this morning. She had put it on top of Nancy's desk before the bell rang — and it was not there now!

Bill looked slyly at Carol and said, "It must have been Nancy's crayon but she didn't know it."

"Wait a minute," said Miss Gray. "I believe I know who stepped on the crayon."

Everyone was looking at everyone else.

"No, don't look at your neighbor. Everyone look at the soles of your own shoes."

Bill was sitting on his foot and as he looked down he saw a streak of red on the bottom of his shoe.

"I didn't know I had stepped on it," said Bill excitedly. "Honest, I didn't Miss Gray. I was in a hurry to get to my seat before the bell rang and didn't even notice it."

Miss Gray laughed.

"All right, Bill. At least that solves the mystery, doesn't it? And does anyone see any reason for being angry at anyone else?"

The children started laughing and all agreed that no one should be punished.

"I think you had art class, Miss Gray, just to help us find out what really happened," said Lucy.

Suggested Discussion Questions
1. What did the children think should be done when they first saw the smashed crayon?
2. Why was Miss Gray interested in finding out who did it?
3. How did Miss Gray find out what had happened?
4. What do you think about Miss Gray's way of finding out what happened?
5. How did the boys and girls feel when they found out how the crayon had been smashed? How do you think they now feel about punishing the person?
6. What might have happened after school if Miss Gray hadn't found out what happened?

In addition to the procedures and materials which have been developed to teach principles of causal behavior, the same organization has produced an annotated bibliography of books and stories which contain material pertinent to the understanding of human behavior. Such material, wisely used, permits children to experience vicariously those things which are useful and instructive but which cannot or should not be experienced directly. Literature has a powerful potential impact on the development of attitudes, values, and feelings in children. They can identify with troubled and triumphant characters in stories and learn alternative ways of acting and feeling. The materials contained in the bibliography are described as experimental. The stories are appropriate for primary and intermediate school children. Each selection specifies the behavior emphasized, gives a summary of the story, and lists appropriate and penetrating questions for use by the teacher. This handbook is also published by the Educational Research Council of America and is titled, *The Causal Approach to Human Behavior Through Literature*.

Research on the effectiveness of the causal approach to teaching behavioral principles has been more extensive than on any other single program in this field. As in many areas of human behavior, certainty is hard to come by, and data are often ambiguous and obscure. However, in general, it seems safe to conclude that children who have been exposed to the program do learn a great deal about human behavior, manifest less punitive and more democratic attitudes, and have a greater tolerance for ambiguity (Ojemann, 1967).

The causal approach to teaching and understanding principles of human behavior has been expanded in scope in recent years to include content dealing with the growing concerns about modern developmental tasks of young people. Changing moral values of society, expanded life styles of individuals, and patterns of social behavior have posed some new challenges. Ojemann (1972) has reflected this changed emphasis by the addition of the word "potential" to his program materials. The program is now known as *Education in Human Behavior and Potential*. The addition of "potential" suggests a new emphasis and recognition of additional possibilities in such a program. Aspects of concerns in the program now include:

1. The teaching of values
2. The guidance of one's own learning
3. Behavior toward drugs
4. Constructive approaches to aggressive and violent behavior
5. Human sexuality
6. Preparation for marriage and parenthood
7. Parent education
8. Mental health education.

To accomplish the objectives covered under these topics, a variety of experiences are discussed and presented in an organized way for use. This includes teacher training programs, narratives, role playing, expositions on factors in complex human behavior, demonstrations, and identity opportunities furnished by teaching examples. Finally, directions for the utilization of effective classroom technique and productive peer interaction processes are described.

The chart on the following pages is a good, concise summary of the objectives' scope and general organization of the program. It also indicates the developmental emphasis and sequence of skills at the various age levels of the child. Presently materials are available for the elementary school. However, it is the intention of the authors to develop appropriate program content for the high school as well. This chart shows the logical sequence of the development of content from the preschool through the twelfth grade level.

FOCUS ON SELF-DEVELOPMENT

"FOCUS is a developmental program designed for use in the classroom by the classroom teacher. The overall objectives of FOCUS are to lead the child toward an understanding of self, an understanding of others, and an understanding of the environment and its effects [Anderson, Lang and Scott, 1971]".

The authors of the FOCUS program believe that children who successfully master key developmental tasks in social and emo-

Scope and Sequence Chart: Education in Human Behavior and Potential*

Category	Pre-school	Kinder-garten 1 2 3	Level 4 5 6 7 8	9 10 11 12
1. Differences between arbitrary, judgmental (S) and causal (C) approaches to behavior and the importance of these differences		At preschool and primary levels pupil learns difference and importance in simple situations	In successive grade or developmental levels more complex situations are considered	In junior and senior years in high school student examines extent of causal orientation in society and how to interact with it
2. Nature of behavior A. Factors producing behavior (Role of motivational feelings, physiological and psychological resources, and immediate physical setting) B. Effects of behavior (includes role of effects in human development)		Growth in awareness of complexity of behavior in simple situations	Develops an elementary systematic plan for considering needs, alternatives, and effects.	Rounds out systematic plan for organizing knowledge of dynamics of behavior
3. Basic "needs," or motivational forces (Includes identification, role in human development, alternative ways of working them out, and estimating probable effects of alternatives)		Learns to talk about and get help when fears, frustrations, boredom become difficult to handle	Identify major motivational feelings or needs, effect of blocking, role of alternatives and examination of consequences, self-examination of motivational growth, and devising developmental measures	Identify extent of fear, worry, boredom, quality of reactions to frustration in society at large, and suggest constructive interaction
4. Methods for getting to know people (Learning about people) A. Direct B. Indirect		Observations of simple individual differences and elementary consideration of accuracy of observations	Systematic study of accuracy of observations, use of tests, and other examining procedures, reports from others, problem of adequacy of sample	Examination of use and quality of observations in society at large, awareness of accuracy of observations, and adequacy of sample, use of second-hand reports
5. Methods for learning about self	Application of simple observation and test methods to self, interpretation of results		Systematic study of observations, self-report, test methods for learning about self, use of results in learning to know self and guiding own development	Methods for monitoring self-development in and out of school

* From Ralph H. Ojemann, Education in human behavior in perspective. *People Watching*, Spring 1972, pp. 60-62. Reprinted by permission.

Scope and Sequence Chart: Education in Human Behavior and Potential (*continued*)

Category	Pre-school	Kinder-garten	Level 1 2 3	4 5 6 7 8	9 10 11 12
6. Learning how to learn (Essentially learning to make decisions as to objective desired and effective experiences for reaching it)			Learning to ask questions about importance of school work, getting help when difficulties arise when beyond one's capabilities to handle	How direct and vicarious explanations affect people, how teacher and pupil work together to make objectives meaningful, learning to use pretests, methods to monitor ones growth, selecting learning experiences	Importance of continuing learning beyond school, facilities in addition to school, methods for monitoring one's development in and out of school
7. Developing language			How to find needed new words when they are needed, importance of listening and clear articulation	The role of new words, how to find them, how direct and vicarious experiences affect language development	Difference in language and sub-language, examining efficiency of language for various purposes, role of language in human development
8. Making moral decisions			(See Category #1)	Developing proficiency in devising alternatives and examining as to effects	Learning methods moral philosophy suggests for developing life purpose, clarifying life goal, and applying it in selecting effects

9. Behavior of adults
A. Behavior of adults as related to the school
  1. Behavior of society in establishing a school
  2. Behavior of teacher and other educational personnel
B. Behavior of parents and guardians
C. Behavior of adults generally
			Early steps in taking a causal approach to behavior of teachers, other school personnel, home environment	Examining one's attitude toward school, authority, interpret results, and planning programs for redirection	Attitude toward authority, role of authority in human development, nature of intelligent cooperation, dynamics of adult behavior in present culture

Scope and Sequence Chart: Education in Human Behavior and Potential *(continued)*

Category	Pre-school	Kinder-garten 1 2 3	Level 4 5 6 7 8	9 10 11 12
10. Behavior of peers	(See Category #1)		Practicing causal approach in room council	Examining behavior of peers out of school, practicing causal approach in daily school and out of school interactions
11. Behavior of selected groups A Younger persons B. Persons in authority C. Persons in subordinate positions D. Minorities	Practicing causal understanding approach in simple situations in school and on playground		Practicing causal understanding in daily situations in and out of school	Study of quality of human interaction in present culture, developing constructive interactions
12. Problems of living in present culture	(See Category #1)		(See Category #1)	Analysis of dynamics of behavior in social problems and indicated plans for development methods for keeping analysis up to date after leaving school
13. Cultures of the past and human "needs"	(See Category #1)		Applications of causal approach to be studied in social science including history and government	Applications of causal approach to behavior studied in social science including history and government
14. How knowledge about people and human society develops	(See Category #1)		(See Category #1)	Role of observation, analysis, and experiment in building knowledge, participation in simple studies, method for keeping abreast of additions to knowledge
15. Applying probability concepts to behavior dynamics	Use of may, might, etc. in simple situations		Applying systematic study of probability to human problems	Applying systematic study of probability to human problems, consideration of significance of probability thinking throughout life

tional learning will be better equipped to deal with the later problems of adolescence and adulthood. The objectives of the program are based on the goals of affective education as described by Krathwohl and others in their book *Taxonomy of Educational Objectives: Affective Domain* (1964).

Presently there are two available levels of the program. *Stage One, Receiving* is divided into three units: "Awareness," "Willingness to Receive," and "Controlled or Selected Attention." *Stage Two: Responding,* has units that deal with the "Personal Self," "Environmental Influences," and the "Social Self." The materials provided for the lesson activities include color filmstrips, accompanying records, story records, two sided photoboards, a copy of the pupil activity book, *Here I Am,* and the teaching guide. Questions are provided as a guide for discussion of each unit and suggested activities are included along with an annotated list of children's books, films, and other material relevant to the theme of the unit.

The general aim of Stage One of the program is directed toward helping children develop awareness of their relationships to others and helping them to learn how to express themselves and their particular "style" and feelings in a context of mutual respect. Children learn to appreciate their uniqueness and to know what their particular "style" of behaving is like and how it affects others. Each of the separate units centers on a particular developmental task.

The FOCUS units for Stage One, in the order of probable use can be seen in this chart reprinted from the Guide for the program.

Topical Arrangement of FOCUS Units*

	Situation or Comment	Unit	Theme Activity
Attributes of Self	Physical self	A	Cindy and the Elf
	Intellectual self	B	Learning in the Park
	Emotional self	C	Circle of Feelings
	Social self	D	Lonesome Ben
Family Relationships	Siblings	B	Learning in the Park
	Parents	D	Lonesome Ben
	Siblings, mother	J	Palmer, the Pushy Pigeon
	Siblings	K	When You're Older, Susie
	Siblings, parents	N	Focus on Sharing
	Siblings, parents	O	Andy, A Boy Who Ran Away
	Siblings	P	Judy's Ups and Downs

*From FOCUS ON SELF-DEVELOPMENT, Stage One: Awareness. © 1970, Science Research Associates, Inc. Reprinted by permission of the publisher.

Under- standing Others (not in family)	Group members	I	The Parade
	Study of one person	L	Photoboards No. 26, 27, 28
	Problems of others	M	A Suggested Approach to Problem Solving
	Seeing both sides	N	Focus on Sharing
	Seeing both sides	P	Judy's Ups and Downs
	Seeing both sides	Q	It Takes Two to Seesaw
	Reasons for behavior of others	R	Do You Know What Happened?
Feelings	Introduction to feelings	C	Circle of Feelings
	Feeling alone or left out	D	Lonesome Ben
	Various feelings	K	When You're Older, Susie
	Various feelings	L	Photoboards No. 26, 27, 28
	Feeling involved in problem solving	M	A Suggested Approach to Problem Solving
	Feelings involved in sharing	N	Focus on Sharing
	Various feelings	O	Andy, a Boy Who Ran Away
	Feeling happy, afraid, angry	P	Judy's Ups and Downs
Sensory Perception of the Environ- ment	Hearing	E	The Sound Machine
	Seeing	F	The Magic Glasses
	Smelling and tasting	G	Tony's Way-Out Nose
	Touching	H	The Blind Men and the Elephant
Problem Solving and Decision Making	How a group might solve a problem	H	The Blind Men and the Elephant
	Various problems to solve	M	A Suggested Approach to Problem Solving
	Sharing problems to solve	N	Focus on Sharing
	Possible consequences of decisions	O	Andy, A Boy Who Ran Away
	Factors leading to problems	P	Judy's Up and Downs
	Causes of problems	R	Do You Know What Happened?

Sharing	Sharing time	D	Lonesome Ben
	Sharing activities	I	The Parade
	Sharing time, things	J	Palmer, the Pushy Pigeon
	Sharing problems to solve	M	A Suggested Approach to Problem Solving
	Study of sharing	N	Focus on Sharing
	Sharing time, space	O	Andy, a Boy Who Ran Away."

The first unit of Stage One deals with attributes of the physical self. Since the child's body is probably the most familiar and non-threatening aspect of him/herself, this seems like a good choice for an introductory activity. This unit contains an overview of the story to be used and suggests dialogue that the teacher may employ in introducing the unit. One of the recorded stories (Cindy and the Elf) is then played. In this story, Cindy is confronted by the elf with the fact that although he may look strange to her, he is like other elves and that in fact, she looks strange to him. Alfred, the elf, then presses her to see if she knows how she looks to other people.

The story is followed by questions designed to help children reflect on how they look to others and to realize outstanding physical attributes of their own appearance. The remainder of the unit is given to suggestions for art work, role playing, games, and various activities that enhance the child's comprehension of his physical self. The unit concludes with a bibliography of books on the theme of the unit.

Stage Two: Responding, has been described briefly. Since Stage Two is designed to elicit positive activity, building on concepts established through the Stage One activities, it should be started rather early in the year providing for material reinforcement of the units.

The logical order of presentation of the units, along with a brief description of the focus and theme activity of the units, shows their sequence and relationship to other parts of the program.

Topical Arrangement of FOCUS Units*

Topic	Unit	Focus	Theme Activity
Feelings	A	Self-Concept	A Very Important Question
	E	Concerns	Handy, My Friend
	F	Responsibility	Second Stringer
	K	Honesty	The Hardest Thing in the World

* From FOCUS ON SELF-DEVELOPMENT, Stage Two: Responding, © 1971, Science Research Associates, Inc. Reprinted by permission of the publisher.

	L	Companionship	Better than Anything
	M	Acceptance/ Rejection	Lynn's Next Move
	N	Respect	Someone Else's Shoes
Family Relationships	C	Abilities/ Limitations	I Can Do Something You Can't Do
	F	Responsibility	Katie All the Way
	G	Physical Environment	Someplace to Go
	I	Social Influences	Copycat
	J	Communication	Communication
	L	Companionship	Better than Anything
	N	Respect	Someone Else's Shoes
Peer Relationships	F	Responsibility	Second Stringer
	G	Physical Environment	Someplace to Go
	H	Cultural Differences	Children Discuss Their Cultures
	I	Social Influences	Copycat
	J	Communication	Communication
	K	Honesty	The Hardest Thing in the World
	L	Companionship	Better than Anything
	M	Acceptance/ Rejection	Lynn's Next Move
	O	Trust	Moving Day for Rufus
	P	Loyalty	One of the Gang
	Q	Competition/ Cooperation	Number One
Problem Solving	F	Responsibility	Second Stringer
	G	Physical Environment	Someplace to Go
	J	Communication	Communication
	M	Acceptance/ Rejection	Lynn's Next Move
	N	Respect	Someone Else's Shoes
	P	Loyalty	One of the Gang
World of Work	B	Interests	A Knapsack of Interests
	C	Abilities/ Limitations	I Can Do Something You Can't Do
	D	Goals	What You Want You'll Get"

Stage Two provides a framework for the child to exercise the competencies and understanding he/she has gained through experiences with the earlier phase of the FOCUS program. As such, it is more active in emphasis and more experiential in the deeper sense of the term. Children are to learn about themselves and how and why they and their friends react as they do. Opportunities are provided to experience new and more satisfying ways of responding.

The Focus of FOCUS

Like most behavioral-experiential teaching programs, the effectiveness of FOCUS in attaining its objectives has yet to be demonstrated adequately. The research that would definitely answer the validity question has not yet been done. However, on the basis of face validity, the FOCUS program appears to be particularly well-planned, based on sound theory, and effectively organized. The materials are of superior quality and the range and scope of furnished plans and suggested activities is especially broad. The grade levels for unit use is not specified and it is apparently left to the experience of the user to determine the most appropriate grade and grouping practices for its use.

The FOCUS program rests on a sound theoretical basis in its attempts to translate the *Taxonomy of Educational Objectives: Affective Domain* into experiential activities in a sequentially structured series of experiences. While it appears that the authors have done a sound job in their efforts, the proof of the effectiveness of the program will be ultimately determined by how well classroom teachers respond to its use. The program can be employed by counselors and school psychologists in their developmental work with children. One of the possible uses of selected units, not suggested by the authors, might be in therapeutic work with small groups of children troubled by common developmental handicaps or school learning and behavioral problems. The possible therapeutic use of the FOCUS program with disturbed and disturbing children may well be profitably explored.

Developing Understanding of Self and Others

The *Developing Understanding of Self and Others*, or DUSO program (Dinkmeyer and Ogburn, 1974) is designed to be used with elementary grade children to accomplish the task suggested by its name. Developed by Don Dinkmeyer, the DUSO kit is a professionally presented, well-organized, structured series of exercises designed to help children develop realistic, positive concepts of themselves. Dinkmeyer believes that the major cause of poor achievement, low aspiration, and unproductive conduct is to be found in the defective concept of self held by problem children.

The series of activities described in the program are aimed at accomplishing positive self-concept changes in eight major behavioral areas. Each unit of the program deals with one of these themes:

1. *Understanding and accepting self.* Children are given an opportunity to see themselves realistically and to become sensitive to their assets as well as their liabilities.
2. *Understanding feeling.* Becoming aware of feelings is stressed in this unit. Children have experiences of positive and negative emotions and learn how these feelings affect behavior.
3. *Understanding others.* This unit is designed to break down the isolation and lack of empathy that retard good relationships.
4. *Understanding and independence.* Developing self-reliance and independence from authority is stressed.
5. *Understanding goals and purposeful behavior.* This unit stresses the value in planning and the penalities of lack of confidence and fear of failure.
6. *Understanding mastery, competence, and resourcefulness.* Children learn to relate desire and ability to competency and achievement in this unit.
7. *Understanding emotional maturity.* Children learn to recognize immature behavior, how it is learned, and how it affects them. They explore the positive uses of emotions and feelings.
8. *Understanding choices and consequences.* Children learn the reciprocal relationship between behavior and outcome and how feelings and values influence what they do.

The three specific objectives which are established for the program and which are found as goals in all eight units are: (1) to learn more ways to describe feelings; (2) to learn the interactive relationship between feelings, goals, and behavior; and (3) to learn to be open to the experience of behavior and feelings. The units are designed so that children can learn these affective principles through experiential learning and examples as well as vicariously through stories and songs.

Dinkmeyer and Ogburn (1974) stress that the programs focus on these developmental tasks:

1. Developing self-identity, self-acceptance, and feelings of adequacy.
2. Learning a reciprocal pattern of affection with peers and parents.
3. Learning to develop mutuality, moving from being self-centered to effective peer, parent-child and teacher-child relations.

4. Learning to become reasonably independent, to develop self-control.
5. Learning to become purposeful, to seek the resources and responsibilities of the world, to become involved, and to respond to challenge with resourcefulness.
6. Learning to be competent, to achieve, to think of self as capable of mastery.
7. Learning to be emotionally flexible and resourceful.
8. Learning to make value judgments, choices, and to accept the consequences of one's choices.

Each of the DUSO units is designed to extend over a period of four to five weeks. The eight units will cover the approximate time available in one school year when offered on a daily basis. Each unit has an introductory story and a song which focuses on the theme. The total unit is comprised of the following activities:

1. A story and discussion
2. Presentation of a program situation and discussion
3. Role playing
4. Puppet activity
5. Supplementary activities and suggestions
6. Recommended supporting reading material

The DUSO kit contains a variety of materials and activity aids. Included are:

1. two story books containing 41 stories, illustrated records or cassettes with two songs and narration of the 41 stories.
2. 33 posters — main points of story are illustrated.
3. puppets — including Duso, who is a listener and helper, and Flopsie who is indecisive and uncertain.
4. hand puppets — sufficient for typical family group.
5. props — cars, clocks, doors, etc.
6. 33 role playing cards.
7. group discussion cards — giving five rules of good discussion.

These materials are packaged attractively, are well designed, and the art work is excellent. Details and specific instructions for use contained in the manual are clear and concise with down-to-earth, understandable language.

With permission of the publisher, we reproduce one of the stories used to introduce a unit to primary students. The illustrations and format are not identical to the publisher's edition due to space and printing limitations. This story is designed to introduce the task of positive self-concept development.

The Red and White Bluebird*

Purpose

Every child's world revolves around himself. The child's first step toward reckoning with the world around him is to know himself. He needs to develop a realistic concept of himself, learning to accept his capabilities in physical, mental, social, and intellectual areas.

In this story, Duso meets a fancy-feathered red and white bird who wants to be a bluebird. Duso helps the bird to see the importance of just being himself. Utilize the story and discussion to accomplish the same objective for each child: you are the only one in the world exactly like you.

Story

Hello, boys and girls. This is Duso the Dolphin, again, with a story for you. One day as I was swimming near the pier, I saw something that surprised me. It was something that I had never seen before! Sitting on top of the pier was the strangest bird that I had ever seen.

The bird had a long yellow head and big yellow feet. It was covered with fancy feathers of red and white squares. It certainly was an unusual bird. I had never seen one like it, even in pictures.

There was one thing that I noticed right away. The bird seemed to be very sad. I always want everyone to have a wide smile so I asked the red and white bird, "Are you sad?"

"Sad!" said the bird. "I am not sad. I am happy. Why should a beautiful bluebird like me ever be sad?"

Something sounded strange. Anybody could see that this was not a bluebird. "Well, isn't that interesting? I think you look red and white," I said.

"No, I am a beautiful bluebird. Look, I will prove it to you."

The bird flew over to a little blue tricycle that was sitting on the pier. She sat on the blue handlebar, looked back at me and said, "Now do you see? I am the same color as this blue tricycle."

She looked just as red and white as before, and that is just what I told her.

So the bird flew out to the end of the pier. She perched on top of a blue bell and called, "Look, I am exactly the same color as this lovely blue bell."

"Oh?" I answered. "You look red and white to me."

The bird just wouldn't listen. She flew back up to the pier and said, "Think of the blue, blue water in the oceans. That is exactly the color I am."

"Well," I said, "you still look red and white to me."

But the bird wasn't listening. She closed her eyes and said, "I am blue . . . blue!"

* From Don Dinkmeyer, *Developing Understanding of Self and Others, Book 1: Stories.* Circle Pines, MN: American Guidance Service, Inc., © 1970. Reprinted by permission of the publisher.

"Why do you want to be blue?" I asked.

"Because everyone likes bluebirds," the bird answered.

"Don't you feel that people like red and white birds?"

The little bird just shook her head, and a big tear started to fall from her eye.

I told her, "Being blue is fine for bluebirds, but you look your best in red and white! And beside that, you are probably the only red and white checkered bird in the whole world!"

My words made the bird feel much better. Then I did something that brought a big smile to the bird's long yellow face — I gave the bird a fancy blue and orange button. On the button were the letters M-E, which spell ME.

"Remember," I said to the bird, "you are the only one like you in the whole world."

Feelings and Words to Talk About

unusual	*happy*
sad	*smile*

What was unusual about the red and white bluebird? What is another word that means the same as unusual?

How did the bird feel when she met Duso? How can you tell when someone is sad? Can each of you wear a sad face for a moment? Good, I can see you know what it means to look sad. How did the bird feel at the end of the story? Do you think she still looked the same? How do you look when you're happy? Let me see you wear a happy face. I see most of you wearing a smile. What does a smile mean? Can you think of a time when you felt happy? Then you know how the bird felt. How did Duso help the bird to be happy? He helped the bird know it was all right to be different. Do you know anyone in the world exactly like you?

The teacher is reminded that as an alternative to the above questions she may wish to:

1. Encourage the children to discuss the feelings and events in the story.
2. Encourage the children to discuss how they might feel and what they might do in a similar situation.

The DUSO materials and programs have been field tested extensively. Over 4,000 children in 166 classrooms have participated in the program. There is no report available in the manual on evaluative research on the program although such reports are beginning to appear in the professional literature.

This program looks promising as a method of teaching behavioral principles to young children. It can be used by teachers without extensive preparation, and it is well-organized and attractively packaged. The rationale and structure of the activities are based on sound knowledge of the developmental needs of children and it appears that they are geared to the appropriate cognitive and interest level of the young school child. It is not, and doesn't pretend to be, an integrated part of the regular subject matter curriculum of the school. This fact is at the same time, one of its strengths and one of its potential weaknesses. Some teachers simply cannot see the value of using their limited "instructional" time for non-academic teaching activities.

The outcomes and effectiveness of the program remain to be seen. The usefulness and effectiveness of the DUSO materials will rest ultimately on how users of the kits feel about the program's effectiveness and on the subsequent research findings relating to self-concept development, affective growth, and behavioral change in the children who are exposed to it.

Additional Program Developments and Resources

We have described several programs of psychological education for elementary children in some detail. Those programs have been developed and organized in a rather comprehensive fashion with activity and instructional elaborations that make them attractive as potential curriculum units. Programs such as FOCUS, DUSO and the *Teaching Program in Human Behavior and Mental Health* are, in reality, packaged and complete instructional units. With minor exceptions, these materials can stand alone as adequate programmatic offerings in behavioral science education for the young school child. Some of the other programs that have been discussed are not as comprehensive. Many would require additional materials and added efforts at integration into other subject areas. Some, such as *TA for Children*, are essentially descriptions of the expansion of a technique of instructional methodology which lends itself to use in the classroom without additional materials but which do require an extensive familiarity and adherence to the concepts and theory on which the technique is based.

One of the most impressive attempts to develop a program and a functional structure for the teaching of psychological principles to children is reported in the book, *Toward Humanistic Education: A Curriculum of Affect* (1970). This book, edited by Gerald Weinstein and Mario D. Fantini and supported by the Ford Foundation, reports on a project to develop effective materials for teaching children from poor, minority group families. The project staff members determined that cognitive learning materials alone were inadequate to the task of providing educational experiences and knowledge necessary for the full development of such children.

They also determined that affect-based programs and materials were necessary to really do the job. As they put it, "Significant contact with pupils is most effectively established and maintained when the content and method of instruction have an affective basis."

Finally, they were convinced, as one outcome of their teaching efforts, that such an approach to the education of the child was necessary for all children and not limited to the special needs of poor and minority group children.

The Humanistic Education staff determined that most traditional education practices were at least partially irrelevant for these reasons:

1. Teaching procedures were not correlated with children's learning styles.
2. Teaching material was often outside the learner's knowledge and experience.
3. Materials and methods often were used that ignored the learner's feelings.
4. Content was irrelevant to the concerns of the learner.

Their efforts were directed toward the use of an affect-based curriculum combined with psychologically enhancing methods of teaching. The effective development of this kind of program would, in the view of the project staff, nullify these four major deterrents to a growth-enhancing educational experience.

The staff employed a wide range of activities, methods, and media to teach the behavioral content they saw as essential to the affective development of the child. One well-known activity, which has been widely reported in the popular press, was the discrimination exercise against blue-eyed children. Another was the use of "self" booklets employing Polaroid photographs to teach positive self-concept. The "one-way glasses" technique developed by Gerald Weinstein required children to wear special glasses that were associated with a particular psychological orientation such as "suspicious," "friendly," or "angry." In the resulting activities, children learned that what they feel affects how they perceive things and how they and others around them behave and respond.

A host of other techniques, methodologies, and materials are reported in the book including the "Them and Us" activity; "Chairs," a subself-concept activity; "The Faraway Island Technique;" "Ten Years From Now;" "Time Capsule;" and finally the integration of diagnosis, concerns and thoughts, culminating in the "Trumpet" model of behavioral interaction. Many of these techniques and methods are well known and are frequently cited in the literature. Others are not so familiar but probably should be known to any educator who plans to develop an affect-based curriculum in his/her school. Most of the activities are fully described in the book and the objectives and special considerations which should be observed in each instance are effectively noted.

The scope of the problem of developing and implementing a program of psychological education for children is descirbed in a concise, definitive manner by Weinstein and Fantini (1970):

> At least 350 major approaches to dealing with psychological growth and some 3,000 affective exercises and techniques have been identified. But the affective-curriculum developer still needs some structures, models, or organizers that will help him to plan for specific outcomes — outcomes that can be clearly communicated to all concerned; that will help him to focus; that will guide his selection of appropriate materials and procedures from the overwhelming number of alternatives that are now available.

Another promising development can be seen in the establishment of new graduate training programs designed to teach ways of developing affect-based curricula and methodology. One such training program in Humanistic Education has been established at the University of Massachusetts. In addition, the New York State Department of Education has begun a program in research and development of psychological education and psychological educators. Many other programs and activities that are related to the educational movement toward attention to the emotional and psychological development of the child have been reported in the literature.

One such program has been developed in the Center Moniches Schools of Long Island, New York. The Human Relations Program, as it is called, is based on materials and methods described in *Toward Humanistic Education* and in the book, *Reach, Touch and Teach* by Terry Borton (1970).

This program relies primarily on discussion techniques and is designed to help children learn to openly express feelings; to recognize and accept others' feelings; to consider the effects of behavior on others; to learn problem-solving methods; and to resolve conflicts in feelings and values. Other activities employed, in addition to discussion, included the "Telephone Game," "Self Searching," and the "Blind and Silent Walk." The description of this program was given by Robert Grussi, school psychologist in a mimeographed paper dated May 12, 1972.

Schulman, Ford and Busk (1973) report on a program to improve the self-concept of children based on the assumptions that (1) the school teaches all children, (2) childhood is the most fruitful growth time, and (3) teachers are natural and best agents to operate such a program.

This project, which was implemented in metropolitan Chicago area schools, involved 6th, 7th and 8th graders. This is the authors' outline of the lessons, including a brief description of the classroom activities involved:

A CLASSROOM PROGRAM TO IMPROVE SELF-CONCEPT*

Appendix A. Self-concept Unit Lesson Plans

Lesson	Focus of the Lesson	Class Activities
I	To familiarize students with the meaning of "self-concept" through an objective study of how other people see themselves and how their opinions affect behavior. Students also will be encouraged to deal with these issues in a personal manner by identifying with these people	Discussion of the opinions that the boy in the film clip has about himself, and the rewriting of the ending of the film.
II	Students continue to evaluate how other people see themselves and how such opinions are demonstrated in a person's behavior, in order to differentiate between a positive and a negative self-concept.	Discussion of the boy's behavior in the film clip as an indicator of his opinion of himself, and the five people outside of class with a classification of their self-concepts as positive or negative.
III	Students continue to evaluate how other people see themselves and how such opinions are demonstrated in a person's behavior.	Discussion of a boy's bragging behavior as an indicator of his opinion and a discussion of the observation of the behavior of five people.
IV	To determine how other people may influence the opinions we have about ourselves.	Discussion of a film clip and the writing of a composition based upon the theme of the clip.
V	Continue discussion of how other people may influence the opinions we have about ourselves.	Continuation of the activities of the previous lesson.

* From J. L. Schulman, R. C. Ford, and P. Busk. A classroom program to improve self-concept. *Psychology in the Schools*, 1973, 10(4), p. 487. Reprinted by permission.

VI	Discussion of "self-acceptance" and how a realistic self-concept depends upon the acceptance of achievement, limitations and failures.	Discussion of whether the boy in the film clip accepted his limitations. Student discussion of their good points and bad points.
VII	To determine the student's appraisal of his self-concept.	The writing of a description of his self-concept by each student and what improvements he would like to work on.
VIII	Students continue to discuss self-acceptance and what constitutes a realistic self-concept.	Continuation of the activities of the previous lesson.
IX	To determine how our self-concept is affected by peer acceptance, adult reaction to us, and family acceptance.	Discussion of how other people influence a boy's opinion of himself and a discussion of an assignment dealing with peer, adult and family influence.
X	Continuation of a discussion to determin how our self-concept is affected by peer, adult and family influence and acceptance.	Discussion of film clip involving a father's influence over a boy's actions and how the boy behaves and feels about himself.
XI	Continuation of a discussion to determine how our self-concept is affected by peer, adult, and family influence and acceptance.	Discussion of a film clip involving a new boy at school and how other students order him around.
XII	To determine how a person can often choose more than one way of acting.	Students and classmates evaluate their opinions of themselves and evaluate their classmates' opinions of themselves and then compare these two ratings.

The experimental conclusions of the results of the program were somewhat uncertain, although it seemed that there were positive changes in the way students saw themselves and in their ability to deal with interpersonal relationships. The teachers reported that the children responded enthusiastically to the program and that they developed new insights and understanding of feelings and behavior.

Other activities, programs, theories, references, techniques and substantive descriptions of psychological educational efforts which should be known by educators who are interested in the affective development of the child include:

1. The May 1973 issue of the *Personnel and Guidance Journal:* This issue is entitled "Psychological Education: A Prime Function of the Counselor," and is a very useful description of the philosophy and practice of psychological education. It contains an excellent orientation to the field as well as program descriptions, references and suggested materials.

2. Systematic Human Relations Training as developed by Robert R. Carkhuff in his book, *Helping and Human Relations, Volumes I and II* (1969): Although the focus of these books is on helping relationships in the more usual clinical settings, the methodologies and techniques could be most effectively used by teachers in fostering the psychological growth of children. Carkhuff has shown conclusively that the interpersonal effectiveness of the most naive person can be dramatically improved with a discrete series of specified learning experiences taught in a systematic, prescribed manner.

3. The book *Learning to Feel — Feeling to Learn* (1971) by Harold C. Lyon, Jr., subtitled *Humanistic Education for the Whole Man,* is based primarily on the theories of Carl Rogers and his contemporaries, such as Abraham Maslow and Frederick Perls, in the humanistic education movement. This book contains a full description of games, exercises and activities contributing to the understanding of emotions and behavior. In addition, it represents an ambitious attempt to provide a psychologically sound, theory-based, structure to the affective educational movement.

4. The Institute for Personal Effectiveness in Children offers training programs for teachers designed to equip them to teach the *Human Development Program* in their schools. The HDP material includes a theory manual, "Magic Circle" activity and story booklets, 180 daily activities and lesson guides, as well as behavioral rating scales for evaluation. The program was developed initially for grades one through six but has now been expanded to cover junior and senior high students. Further information is available from Human Development Training Institute, 4455 Twain Avenue, Suite H, San Diego, California 92120. A description of the use of the *Human Development Program* methods and materials is reported by Levine (1973). She states that

utilization of the HDP program activities resulted in improved warmth and openness in the classroom; a greater empathy on the part of involved teachers with increased sensitivity to the affective life of their students; and a more productive, pleasant teaching atmosphere. Materials and activities from *Education for Success* by L. Sewell (in press), were also used.

5. The use of children's literature in developing behavioral competencies is reported by Patricia Cianciolo in *Personnel and Guidance Journal* (May, 1965). In her article, "Children's Literature Can Affect Coping Behavior," Cianciolo stresses the employment of dramatic literature in therapeutic and developmental work with children. She suggests that the effective use of such materials, in conjunction with other activities, can facilitate the psychological processes of identification, cartharsis, and insight. Over 60 pertinent stories are listed and described with notation as to their usefulness with varying age groups.

6. In their book, *Reality Games* by Sanville Sax and Sandra Hollander (1972), many activities are described that are "game structured" and which are designed to increase awareness and coping behavior. Over 50 games are described in detail, many of which are appropriate for use with elementary age children. They include role-playing games, sensitivity games, body awareness games, and games to enhance coping and relating behaviors. Although this book is aimed at an adult audience, the creative teacher will find a number of activities and exercises for use with elementary age children.

7. Albert Ellis (1962 and 1971) has extended the theories and practices of his system of psychotherapy to the education of the young child in the Living School in New York City. These children are taught the emotional, cognitive, and behavioral methods of living as developed in his system of rational-emotive psychology. A full treatment of this program is described in Ellis' books.

8. Bob Valett, a prolific writer on the subject of handicapped children, child development, and school psychology, has authored a new work on affective education. His book, *Affective-Humanistic Education: Goals, Programs, and Learning Activities* (1974) is designed to help administrators develop viable, affect-based curricular experiences and programs. Valett has also produced a workbook for

student use, *Getting It All Together* (1974), which contains a series of affective-emotive lessons.

9. The Minnesota Department of Education (Miller, 1973) has published an excellent survey of affect-oriented educational programs and activities including appropriate content aimed at work with children, with teachers, and with parents. Their report includes descriptions of programs designed to produce positive self-concept change in children as well as activities aimed at enhancing communication processes and peer understanding. Particular attention is given to the role of the elementary counselor in psychological education. The book includes an overview of concepts of affective development and gives examples of instructional materials and evaluation procedures. Emphasis on planning and organizing is stressed, and the editor of the report, G. Dean Miller, repeats the advice given by others who have become involved in initiating and operating instructional programs of this nature.

> It is important to note that in most all of the research reported herein the positive influence of counselor led activities is a result of some designated competence applied in a systematic way to a specific need of children, teachers, or parents. It appears that psychological education, like cognitive learning, is most successful when learning activities are relevant and presented in an orderly manner over a period of time.

10. Anna Wagner has written a book designed to help the student learn about him/herself and "to face himself and life realistically." The book *Sharing My World — A Course in Human/Personal Development for Elementary Children* (1974) is published with accompanying student workbooks. The "lessons" are a combination of didactic material, group interaction, and experiential exercises. The topics covered include "Me," "Parents," "Siblings," "Other Adults," "Friends," "Plants," "Animals," and finally "Me Again."

The book and accompanying student workbooks are less exploratory and more directive than other programs we have reviewed. The program, in the words of the author, ". . . affords the elementary-age child a full one-year course in positive living." As such, it apparently limits the child's needs to explore and discover aspects of him/herself and of those around him/her that do not contribute to "positive living." Some of the material from this work may be useful in developing a program of psychological education for children. However, it seems rather restricted in its approach to the task and very narrow in scope.

These and other books, articles, and teaching materials have contributed to the trend toward increasing emphasis on the affective development of children in the modern school curricula. Peter Dow (1971) reports that a review of 26 of the better-known recent social studies curriculum projects reveals a profound shift in content emphasis including:

1. from facts to conceptual approaches
2. from traditional social studies to anthropology, sociology, psychology, political science and economics
3. from unilateral to interdisciplinary
4. from facts to values, attitudes, and social realities
5. from deductive to inductive methodologies
6. from provincial to multi-cultural studies

As we noted earlier in this chapter, a wealth of literature, programs and materials on psychological education for the young child is available. Much of it is based on sound theory and is presented clearly and in an organized, understandable manner. Much of the available work in the field however, is based on hunch and fad and is untested and unproven. The educator who is interested in moving into affective education should be wary of the programs offered to him/her and cautious in the methods and techniques he/she adopts. There are well-tested and soundly based programs available and these should form the basis of any new implementation of psycho-educational programs for children by a school system. "Let the buyer beware" is a sound idea to observe.

4

Education and Life

More than half of the hospital beds in our country are occupied by people with mental and emotional ailments. About 20 million people, or one person out of ten, have emotional problems so severe and so distressing that they need to seek help sometime in their lives. In addition, there is growing evidence that most criminals, delinquents, alcoholics, "dead-beats," and drug addicts are victims of emotional reactions that they cannot cope with in a personally or socially satisfying way. Taken all together, the staggering fact is that probably one out of every five people we meet is suffering, or has or will suffer at some time in his/her life from an inability to live satisfactorily with him/herself or others.

Yet, in the face of this picture, we can legitimately take the position that "mental illness" has little to do with the situation! The term "mental illness" has been used to popularize and gain financial and social support for efforts to provide resources to relieve the intense suffering of these many millions whose lives are depressing, or frightening, or boring, or perhaps simply without purpose or pleasure.

Maladaptive Behavior

Most of these unfortunate people are not "ill" in the generally accepted use of the term. They don't suffer from a bacteria or a virus. There's nothing organically wrong with their brains or their endocrine glands. They haven't had their cerebral functions disrupted by head injuries or chemical agents. They are, rather, suffering from disorders of living. That their behavior is caused is true, but not by an agent that is similar to the ones that cause us physical distress. Rather they are impaired by frustrations, by conflicts, and by the failure of society to provide them with the "mental nourishment" which all of us must have to be productive, happy, and fully functioning persons.

Of course, there are a number of distressed persons who are impaired in their ability to live productively who really do suffer from "mental disease." Alcoholism and drugs can, and do, organically impair the brain. People do suffer head injuries and physical illnesses which disrupt their thinking and feeling and behavior. In addition, there is an increasing consensus among authorities in the field that the extremely disrupting conditions that we have labeled psychosis or insanity may require some disordered function of the brain, in addition to poor life experience, to make their appearance.

But still, these factors are not involved in the millions of people who end their marriages by divorce, who can't hold jobs, who live lives of secret despair, who fail in school, who can't form close friendships, or who are constantly impaired in their living by hate and resentment. These millions of our brothers are "sick" because they cannot get the necessary psychological or emotional "food" to sustain themselves. They are people who can't find deep, loving relationships with others and cannot find productive, fulfilling ways to spend their lives.

Needs of Human Beings

Humans are really unique. They are the only animals in the world with a dual need system. They share with other animals the need to satisfy physiological needs. Just like the dog or the monkey, they must have food, water, shelter, and warmth to sustain themselves. Their bodies demand exercise, maintenance of vigor, nourishment, and freedom from disease or they will malfunction, or cease to function.

However, here human beings and other animals part company. Humans need much more than this. In fact, without more than the minimal fulfillment of physiological needs, humans really are little different from other animals. Humans, and there are no exceptions to this, need to think, to feel, to act, to interact, to feel joy, and sometimes pain. They need to be loved, nurtured, and comforted. They need to solve problems, to make things work, to play games. They need to give love and comfort and to nurture others. They want, and must have, respect, friendship, companionship, and intellectual and sensory stimulation. To fulfill their humanity, they need to create, to solve problems, to manage their lives, and to contribute to the lives of others. In short, humans are much more different than they are like other animals. The human being is animal in only a peripheral, superficial way.

What happens to a person who is not nurtured as a child, who is not loved or respected as an adult, or who fails to find a productive, satisfying way to spend his/her days? What kind of a man or woman will the child come to be who has lived in fear, failure, or rejection all his/her life? What happens to the child who is indulged and left to his/her own devices while growing up? What life does the person have who has been denied care and joy and fulfillment as his/her "life style" was being formed?

The answer is of course rather obvious. Such persons become the malcontents, criminals, the neurotics and psychotics that we discussed earlier. In milder cases of deprivation, they become simply unhappy, resentful, or purposeless people who wander through life without goals and without much pleasure, fighting a continuous battle to win enough psychological "food" to simply keep going.

What are these psychological needs that make humankind so vitally different from all other members of the animal kingdom? A psychologist and philosopher named Abraham Maslow (1954) says that humans need basically four kinds of things, aside from physiological requirements to become fully human. These needs are: *safety* and *security*, *love* and *belongingness*, *esteem*, and *self-actualization*.

These psychological needs are, of course, secondary, in a sense, to our physical needs. We would add to Maslow's needs, a more inclusive but perhaps more difficult term to understand in order to encompass esteem and self-actualization. Combs and Snygg (1959), call this term *adequacy*. They define this term by saying ". . . we mean that great driving, striving force in each of us by which we are continually seeking to make ourselves ever more adequate to cope with life."

Achieving Needs

It may be misleading to leave this important term at this point without making one important observation. The word "cope" in Comb's and Snygg's description of adequacy does not really do justice to the meaning of the definition. We all are seeking to deal positively with our world, to use it to develop our abilities and to expand our lives. At times, the best we can do is "cope." But, our goals are beyond merely coping. A psychiatrist named Alfred Adler, founder of a system of human behavior called "Individual Psychology," characterizes this need as a striving for superiority or power. Alder explains that power in this sense is gaining mastery over one's world, not over other people. We will give more detail on this idea later in this chapter.

The first demand we make on our environment is for food, warmth, and bodily integrity. Until those basic needs are satisfied we cannot move to fulfill those uniquely human needs that we call psychological. This is why we can do little to encourage the freedom of the individual until he/she is fed. A hungry mouth does not talk of love, compassion, or learning. It speaks, instead, of meat, potatoes, and milk.

Safety or security is probably the more basic and requisite of the physiological human needs. Everyone needs to feel that he/she is free from danger. The baby needs to feel secure in the arms of the parents. He/she needs some order and routine in his/her young life. He/she must have the security that comes from being able to make reasonable predictions about the way the world operates. Everyone needs a predictable, orderly and organized environment in which to grow.

Most people have a world that is reasonably orderly. Some do not. Their safety is actually in peril. They may be cared for and they may not be. They may be protected from some dangers and carelessly exposed to others. At times in their lives they are left without protectors. Such persons, especially if they are young, will sooner or later show the effects of the failure to provide for their security needs. In children, this may be manifested in crying and clinging behavior, or conversly, in aggressive and demanding attacks. In adults, this lack may be manifested in an anxious approach to everything in life, sometimes to the point of despair, depression or even suicide.

Security is the prerequisite psychological need. The fear of abandonment is the most threatening emotion in the life of a child and will persist throughout the life of the adult if security needs are not met in infancy and childhood. Many delinquent adolescents show evidence of a failure to have these needs satisfied. Although security needs may be neglected more often in poor or in disorganized families, they are often missing in affluent families where parental responsibilities are not met. Sometimes such parents are unable to adequately care for these needs of their children because they themselves did not have their safety needs satisfied.

Children who not only fail to have these minimum needs satisfied but who are actually threatened in their survival through severe physical punishment, brutal treatment, or threats of abandonment show, in later life, the greatest emotional disability. They become in their own time brutalizers of their own children, terrorizers of society, or they give up the struggle for safety in the false refuge of drug abuse, alcoholism or depression and suicide.

A psychologist named Harry Harlow has shown that even infant monkeys suffer irreversible emotional damage when their needs for security are severely and chronically violated. Perhaps the other animals are more like humans than we would care to believe.

Love and Belongingness

The development of a loving and compassionate personality can begin only after the child's needs for physical necessities and security are met. The manifestations of these mere human feelings cannot emerge in a personality that is preoccupied with hunger or with fear. When these needs are reasonably well met, the search will begin for "food" to fill the need for love, accomplishment, and belongingness.

The evidence for the strong, compelling nature of the need to belong is around us everywhere. We feel pity for the orphan, sorrow for the widow, compassion for the refugee. One of the greatest threats that young adults or children can have is to be faced with rejection by their age group. People show every day in their behavior how vital is the need to belong. Sometimes this takes maladaptive forms when they lie, cheat, or abuse others to get or retain attention and affection from others. In the school, we see everyday manifestations of this need in behavioral and learning problems of far too many children.

Some humans, with a very weak hold on others, will involve themselves in every conceivable kind of behavior to gain membership in a valued group. The so-called Manson "family" is a stark example of the lengths to which people will go in order to belong. The drug and "hippy" cultures are, at least in part, maintained because they fulfill, although at a very high price, the needs of humans to belong and to be loved.

Sexual behavior is, in part, a manifestation of the need to love and to commit oneself to others. This need, along with our more purely animal urges, compels us to approach others, to risk a commitment, and to expose ourselves to the possibility of rejection. Again, the power of this love-belonging need is shown in reactions to sexual or affinity rejection. Our literature abounds with tales of remorseful lovers and our newspapers are filled with stories of homicides and suicides precipitated by rejection of proffered love.

Because our sexual needs are a part of our love and belonging needs, we cannot violate one without affecting the other. Essential love commitments cannot be made by one person to everyone in his/her world. The very nature of the concentration of energy and interest in such feelings precludes this. So, when such needs are thwarted or when despair of ever attaining adequate love supplies is felt, desperate means are grasped. Sexual promiscuity is one evidence of such rejection. Contrary to outward appearances, such promiscuity reflects the inability of the person to find a relationship which can satisfy his/her desperate desire to love and be loved, to belong to another, and to have them belong to him/her. Successful school accomplishment is the first step in becoming competent as an adult in filling our needs for mature sexual and affective satisfaction.

There really is no moral imperative that restricts us, very effectively, in our sexual conduct. No admonitions of right or wrong can really provide a meaningful guide for our conduct. Rather, we are guided and compelled by inexorable laws of human behavior. Such laws demand the fulfillment of our needs to belong and to be loved. And we cannot separate sexual behavior from this. This is why sexual "shopping" can never satisfy our deepest needs and why we cannot violate such needs without paying a high price for it in the long run.

Needs Frustrated

Thwarting and frustration of the need to belong and to give and receive love is probably the major cause of destructive behavior and emotional suffering. The basis for the satisfaction of this need must be established early in life. The school must lay the foundation for this. A partial list of the conditions resulting, at least in part, from society's failure to fulfill these needs include

1. criminal activities of all kinds, especially destructive-aggressive acts such as rape, vandalism, sexual molestation, and physical assault. In the classroom, it may take the form of excessive "showing off," teasing, fighting, quarreling.

2. withdrawal activities such as social isolation, chronic depression, extreme shyness and suicide, school failure and poor motivation.
3. searches for "nirvana" or oblivion by such acts as sexual promiscuity, homosexuality, chronic alcoholism and drug addiction.

Some people give up the effort to fulfill their love needs and retreat into isolation or to enter into bitter, quarrelsome relationships with everybody they meet. Some go so far as to create a world that is more acceptable and less threatening and rejecting. They may live out their days in a fantasy of their minds where the possibility of being rejected never exists. The basis for the adult's approach to solving these needs is established in how we satisfy the emotional needs of children as they succeed or fail in their school experiences.

The Need for Adequacy

If our primary needs for physical sustenance, security, and belonging are adequately met in our early lives, we will move on to the fuller development of our humanness as we mature. We will seek to master our world and to shape its form in such a way that it provides us with pleasure and with a feeling of competency and control. We will strive to achieve things which are difficult, yet beautiful or useful. We will begin to act in ways that win respect and even admiration from our friends. We will give of ourselves to others. We will be concerned about others who are weaker, younger, poorer, or less capable than we. We will try to help others find some of what we have found. Our enthusiasm and energy will increase and be replenished by each new task we complete and each new challenge we confront. In short, we will become people who try to make their lives good to themselves and to others. We will become self-actualized or adequate people.

Self-actualized or adequate persons are inner-directed. They don't set their standards of conduct or behavior by what the crowd is doing. They decide what is good for them and that is what they do. They see themselves as persons of value and regard themselves as essentially fair, honest, and worthy. In this feeling about themselves, they believe others regard them positively and relate to others with that expectation. This is as true for the third grader as for the senior citizen.

Individuals with adequate personalities are able to act and react more effectively than others. They can evaluate events and facts clearly and objectively and use the conclusions in guiding their behavior. They are also more spontaneous and more creative. They let experiences happen rather than fighting or resisting. As a result of their inner freedom, new thoughts and new relationships between ideas occur. They will likely see things in a new way with a unique understanding that most of us don't have. They become better students and as they grow, more competent adults.

In their book, *Individual Behavior*, Combs and Snygg (1959), report that E. M. Berger characterizes the adequate person like this:

1. Relies on internalized values and standards.
2. Has faith in capacity to cope with life.
3. Assumes responsibility for and accepts causes of own behavior.
4. Accepts praise or criticism objectively.
5. Does not deny or distort feelings, motives, abilities in self.
6. Sees self as person of worth or as equal to others.
7. Does not expect others to reject him.
8. Does not regard himself as queer or abnormal.
9. Is not shy or self conscious.

Berger (1952) reports that the truly adequate person feels this way about others:

1. Does not hate, reject or pass judgment on others when different from self.
2. Does not attempt to dominate.
3. Does not assume responsibility for others.
4. Does not deny worth or equality of others.
5. Shows desire to serve others.
6. Has active interest in others, desires to create mutually satisfactory relationships.
7. In advancing self, is careful not to infringe rights of others.

Becoming

How far have most of us gotten in acquiring these traits in our own personality and lives? Probably not too far. But, the outstanding characteristic of the adequate personality, at any age, is that of growth. Such people continue to try to be more than they now are. They are in the process of becoming. They may act like fools at times, they may occasionally be mean and cruel, they may shirk some important duty, or lie to avoid an unpleasant truth. But, in the long run, the adequate person, tries again. (S)He resolves to do better next time and does! His failures become fewer as he grows older and his successes more frequent. In truth, he is compelled by the fact of human life as Maslow (1954), put it, "What a man can be, he must be."

It seems obvious that the struggle to be adequate is a task for us all. It is also apparent that the attainment of adequacy is the principal goal of our life: a goal so vital and urgent that we literally will do anything and go to any lengths to achieve it. Of course, nobody achieves "adequacy" in the sense that nobody ever achieves personal perfection. But in one way or another we all strive for it. Children in their own way are striving too, and schools must provide the experiences which will help them to build such feelings.

It is in this "one way or another" that we search for self-esteem, for adequacy, for mastery, for self-actualization that we are concerned about in this chapter. Most of us, most of the time, seek adequacy in personally and socially fulfilling ways. We work or study hard, we try to help and be fair to others. We seek new experiences and try new ways of behaving. We decide for ourselves what is right and wrong. We are kind to weaker, younger, or less powerful people. We think of others when we do things or aim for new accomplishments.

We can do all these things in constructive, self-fulfilling ways because we are free enough from threat and have enough emotional "supplies" to free us from the constraint of fear, rejection, hate, and despair. But many people — at times all of us — are not so free. They suffer the terrific burden of trying to find personal adequacy in the face of overwhelming fear and anxiety or while simultaneously trying to satisfy their physical and safety needs. In short, they cannot free themselves to grow toward adequacy. These people we call inadequate personalities. You can hear them called by other labels such as mentally ill, emotionally disturbed, neurotic or psychotic. Whatever the label, they all suffer from their inability to satisfy their human needs for security, belonging and growth.

Characteristics of People in Distress

People who find themselves victimized by their feelings and behavior are not happy people. Often, they will impress us as overbearing loudmouths. Sometimes they will attempt to bolster their sagging self-esteem by bragging, clowning, and taking unnecessary and foolish risks. As students, they cheat, are disruptive, and become "problems." The one thing that all mentally and emotionally disturbed people have in common is their inability to establish meaningful, productive, and pleasurable relationships with others.

This relationship problem can take many forms, depending on the background and particular circumstances of each individual. It may appear in a fawning, cowering, and martyred attitude. But, it may take the very opposite form as an over-aggressive, authoritative, critical and hostile appearance. Children withdraw, fail to study, and develop emotional aches and pains. The forms and behavior engaged in by people in distress are many and varied, but they all spring from a common source which is the individual's displeasure with himself.

How does a mentally disturbed child or adult see him/herself? According to Combs and Snygg, such persons have three basic personality characteristics.

First, they have a negative self-concept. They see themselves as unlovable and uninteresting. Deep inside they feel that they, and the things they do, are not worth very much. Often they regard themselves as dumb, weak, ignorant, or ugly. The objective picture that you and I see isn't important. To others they may be handsome or beautiful, smart and well-read, and a pleasure to be with. But, in this case, the "facts" don't matter. To them, they are what they feel.

People who feel this way about themselves are resentful and angry. They will probably be belligerent and aggressive though sometimes they are apologetic and excessively shy. Research on the self-concepts of juvenile delinquents has shown that these boys and girls see themselves in such negative terms. They feel stupid, worthless, and unlovable. They can't see themselves as ever being really valued for themselves and can't imagine themselves as "belonging."

A man or woman (or boy or girl) who brags excessively and constantly calls attention to what he can do, has done, or what important relatives and friends he has is suffering from negative feelings about his own worth and value.

A second characteristic of such persons is their lack of acceptance. They not only see themselves as valueless but they expect others to be this way also. They suspect offers of friendship as something designed to take advantage of them. They are suspicious of the motives and feelings that others express. Because of their preoccupation with their feelings of worthlessness and their rejection of others, they can't view the world and the things around them as they really are. They aren't open to new experiences and new learnings. They reject the unique, the unknown, and the strange. As a result of this, they don't have much knowledge and information available to them. Their judgments and decisions are likely to be prejudiced and warped. In fact, any information that comes their way that contradicts the way they see themselves or their world is likely to be rejected.

Constriction

Distressed people have tunnel vision. They see only through a narrow, prescribed funnel. All the other things that are going on in the world around them are ignored or passed by as if they were unimportant. They are so involved in defending their perception of themselves that they have no energy or inclination to look at what others are doing or saying. They note facts and circumstances that confirm what they believe and feel about themselves and ignore everything else. As students, they are constricted, rigid, and unimaginative.

The boy who feels that his parents are picking on him and are out to get him may go for days in relative harmony. His mother may praise him for his help around the house and his father may reward him with use of the car and trips to the ball game for good grades and responsible behavior. But, one remark about the length of his hair or the condition of his room convinces him that his parents are bent on tormenting and harassing him. The facts of the case don't really matter! He feels like he feels and he'll find evidence to confirm his feelings. The same things happen in school to children in their interaction with teachers and fellow students.

A third feature of the behavior of distressed persons is their inability to identify with others. They simply can't see other people as essentially honest, sympathetic and friendly. They really believe that others are cold and critical and they expect them to act that way. When they are confronted, if their behavior will permit it, with the fact that another person has treated them warmly and justly, they wonder what the other person is up to or what game he/she is playing. They often see others as out to use them or take advantage of them.

As a result of this inability to identify with others, troubled persons are often selfish and egocentric. They are proud of their belief in the motto, "Do unto others before they do unto you." Consequently, such people find it impossible to form lasting friendships with others. They may associate, and even appear to be close to someone else. But, when examined closely, the relationship can easily be seen as a competitive struggle with constant effort to maintain the upper hand and control. And of course such people reject any evidence or occurrences that would suggest that other people have integrity or honor, or that they may find fairness and justice with others. You've probably heard such people say things like "All politicians are crooked and everyone of them comes out of public office rich," or "If you don't take care of yourself, nobody else will." The child might feel that the only way to win the "school game" is to cheat.

They justify their own feeling of worthlessness and dishonesty by attributing these values to everyone else. It's as if they say to themselves, "I'm not really so bad after all because that's the way others feel and that's the way the world is run." Of course, the probability that they can be convinced of the value and worth of others is slim unless we provide early growth enhancing experiences in school. Racial and religious prejudice is one of the outcomes of such twisted feelings.

Self-Fulfilling Prophesy

Then our picture of the emotionally disturbed, or distressed adult or child is this: (s)he wants security, love, belonging and self-esteem but can't secure enough of these things to satisfy his needs. He reacts bitterly, fearfully, passively, or belligerently, and sees himself as a worthless, unlovable, powerless person.He can't accept others for what they are or grant them any different motives or feelings than he has himself. Consequently, he sees others as dangerous, cold, uncaring and critical. He selectively gathers "facts" that support his views of himself and others and ignores other data. He is estranged from his family, his friends, his teachers, and most sadly of all, from himself. The old adage "to know thyself" as the basis of personal freedom is valid. But the struggle to know oneself is so very difficult, and sometimes impossible, because the very threat and fear that engender these feelings cause us to close ourselves to experiencing the world as it could be.

How People Defend Themselves Against Threat — the Basis of Personal Failure

We might show the progression of human behavior to a maladaptive conclusion in this way:

Need . . . Thwarting . . . Threat . . . Anxiety . . .
Maladaptive Behavior

You will note that immediately preceeding the behavior we call *emotionally disturbed*, we find the emotion of anxiety. This emotion is the basis for all maladaptive behavior that is caused by psychological dysfunction. Anxiety is that feeling of dread or of impending disaster which in its strongest form is simply intolerable to us. The feeling of anxiety must be distinguished from fear. In fear, our feelings are determined, at least to a degree, by an objective threat. We may be fearful because we think we will fail a test or lose a job. Or we may be afraid on a dark street late at night in a rough part of town. But anxiety differs from this kind of object fear in two very critical ways.

The first distinguishing characteristic of anxiety is its object. What are we anxious about? Generally, we don't really know. We can't clearly describe the source of our anxiety or what real danger it suggests for our lives. We only know we have a vague sense of forboding, an unclear feeling of trouble or even disaster. Sometimes we are so uncomfortable with this feeling that we try to attribute it to something so we can manage it more effectively. Often, the things we attach our fear to for this purpose have no connection at all to the real source of our discomfort. This is often the case when people are apparently needlessly fearful of common objects such as cats or of activities such as riding elevators. In children it often takes the form of poor motivation, reading disorders, or unwarranted aggression against peers.

The second major characteristic of anxiety is its pervasiveness. None of our life space is free from disruption caused by feelings or anxiety.

Our relationships with others as well as our job or school work are corrupted by our anxiousness. Even our times for leisure and play are shadowed by the specture of ever-present anxiety. Of course, the level of discomfort that one experiences and the degree of disruption of one's life depends on the severity of the feeling of anxiety. We all have some anxiety. It is unlikely that a world could be engineered or a life developed that did not leave a residue of anxiety in everyone. In fact, it probably would not be desirable to eliminate all anxiety even if we could.

But anxiety, beyond the mildest levels, is one of the most distressing experiences of living. In its more powerful form, it can cause panic, despair, physical illness, chronic psychological disability, and even death. Persons who are afflicted with a chronic high level of anxiety will eventually display symptoms of maladaptive behavior. The nature of this behavior will be a function of (1) the severity of the anxiety, (2) the life experiences of the individual, and (3) environmental opportunities and limitations. What happens to the child in school can ameliorate anxiety or exacerbate it.

Searching for Competency

Chronic, unrelieved anxiety most often will cause behavioral problems in the psychological meaning of the term. However, anxiety can cause, contribute to, or aggravate, physically disabling conditions. Some of the conditions that are considered to have stress as a major contributing factor to their origin or continuation include peptic ulcer, migraine headaches, asthma, ulcerative colitis, vascular hypertension, epilepsy, and impotency or frigidity. The conditions for the development of these problems may be established or avoided by what we do in the schools to and for children. It has been estimated that about 75% of the patients that the general practicing physician sees have primarily psychological problems or have physical illnesses that are aggravated or confounded by severe psychological complications.

Many of the feelings of fatigue and general "blahs" that we all have from time to time are primarily manifestations of unresolved emotions of which anxiety is the primary culprit. The occasional problems that we have with constipation or diarrhea, shortness of breath, poor appetite, or headaches are likely caused by emotions that we have been unable to resolve or even to bring into full awareness. For most of us, most of the time, these episodes are short, cause no real disruption of our lives, and soon are forgotten. Unfortunately, some people experience such strong and unremitting feelings of distress that they are continually seeking a new medical treatment, doctor, drug, or operation that will relieve their distress. Most of them never find it.

We can help children develop competency, feelings of adequacy and skills that will not only make school a fulfilling experience in itself but that will help them to become adequate adults. What we do in the school to provide the emotional sustenance and care that children need can help them avoid the distress and pain of a later life of physical and psychological stress. Adults don't suddenly become neurotics, hypochondriacs, criminals, or inadequate people; it takes years to develop a constricted, disorganized personality. But it takes no longer to build a happy, productive, satisfying life. To a large degree, it is within the power of the school to determine life's circumstances for its children.

Hindsight and Forecasting

A variety of information, curriculum outlines, program units, instructional aids, and a host of other paraphernalia related to psychological education are available in libraries, publisher's houses, and in the hands of many innovative people. As the reader has seen, the professional literature is filled with theoretical, research and practical articles on the subject. Everyone, including educators, psychologists, counselors, and administrators, supports the notion of providing an educational environment and instructional experiences that enhance psychosocial growth of children. It would be hard to find any responsible spokesman who really opposed the concept of psychological education.

Yet, in spite of protestations and assurances of support, we look around our educational house and we see business carried on much in the way that it was when we were students. True, curriculum content and instructional methodology have improved. Our efforts to establish comprehensive high schools, to offer individualized instruction, to teach career development, and to provide programmed learning materials, as well as a host of other valid innovations, prove that schools have improved markedly in their concerns and practices especially in the realm of substantive-cognitive development of young people. But not too much has really changed in emphasis on the *deliberate* development of psychological competency in students. The mind-boggling and bewildering variety of affect-oriented developmental programs reported in the periodical literature and in the various textbooks is, paradoxically, the very proof of this. It appears that promising programs and innovative ideas in this area flourish for a time and then disappear. Almost always, program initiation and operation can be traced to one or two key individuals who were responsible for the beginnings of the program and its subsequent success; but, when they "move on" or lose interest, the "new" program grinds to a labored halt and soon is forgotten. There are enough pioneers and innovators to keep something going in psychological education somewhere all the time. But, too often these programs are sustained by a dynamic, aggressive personality and when that person disappears, so does the program, even in the face of apparent success.

If this phenomenon is as we have described it, how can we account for such futility and waste? Why do apparently successful programs appear to lose their effectiveness and, after awhile, almost always become abandoned? How can we explain the reluctance of educators to accept the research data on successful behavioral change through such programs? Why aren't curriculum plans developed and incorporated to make *deliberate psychological education* a part of the regular school program for every child?

We cannot pretend to understand or explain all the possible reasons for this phenomenon. Perhaps some of these reasons and resistances were described by Bower (1969) in the first chapter of this monograph. There is, as he points out, a deep reluctance on the part of all of us to deliberately interfere with what we regard as the last refuge of personal privacy, the psyche of the individual. Yet, we know, cognitively, that what we do or don't do in the school affects the psycho-social development of the child. And since we must "do" or "not do" something, our choice is not whether to impact or not on the psychological growth of the child. Rather, our only real choice is to determine *how and in what manner* we will help to shape the character and personality of the child. If we finally accept the inevitable conclusion that what we do *will* unavoidably influence the psychological nature of our students, perhaps then we can accept the responsibility of trying deliberately to make that inevitable impact as productive and fulfilling as we possibly can.

Clouded Goals

This effective and perhaps unconscious reluctance to "tamper" with the personality of children may explain in part the relative failure of the psychological education movement. But, by itself, this is not a sufficient explanation. It may well be that we simply don't know enough about psychological growth to do competently those things that we think need doing on behalf of the emotional development of the child. After all, the structure of the personality and its development, in spite of the millions of words written on the subjects, are not nearly as well understood as the structure of the intellect, of learning, or of factual and substantive knowledge of content areas such as physics, reading, or social sciences.

Maybe our difficulties in planning for the psychological growth of children can be explained, at least in part, by our failure to develop a generally accepted theoretical basis of understanding of the nature of affective development. It is difficult to structure experiences, develop exercises, and incorporate content for an instructional program if we only vaguely understand the nature of the developmental stages of the process we are trying to describe, define, and translate into operational instructional goals. Maybe we really don't know how to teach and expose children to the proper sequence of experiences to achieve the desired outcome! We know what outcome we want. As educators, we want to produce citizens who are productive, happy, and effective in living. A part of our failure then may reflect not our reluctance to try but our ignorance of how to do what we know we need to do.

Cognitive and psychological development processes are usually treated, in our professional literature, as mutually exclusive entities. If you are reluctant to accept that as a fact, simply look at this monograph! We have been compelled, perhaps because of our own limitations in knowledge, to treat the developing child as if he/she were divided into two parts, the intellectual and the psychological or emotional. We know far too little about the inter-dynamic functioning and growth of the "whole child." Dusek

(1974) argues that there is a pressing need to study the relationship between cognitively related developmental levels in children and corresponding affective status. He makes the vitally important point that we know relatively little about the interrelationship of different facets of child development and how one affects the other. It may be possible to understand certain aspects of affective development only in terms of the levels of cognitive understanding or even value judgment competencies that children have mastered. It may well be that our attempts to modify and enhance the growth of the child cannot be effectively divided between programs that are exclusively affective or intellectual in their orientation or focus.

Strategies

Another dichotomy in our efforts to deal with the subject of psychological education is seen in our operational approaches to the task. Strategies employed generally take one of two tacks. We try to either (1) increase the psychologically enhancing skills of the teacher, or (2) to incorporate psychologically relevant instructional materials into the curriculum. Seldom do we see programs which deal with both teacher skills and instructional techniques, as well as curriculum content and experiences.

Most of the programs reviewed in this monograph are examples of change through incorporation of affective content and carefully structured experiences. On the other hand, attempts to impact on the psychological development of the child by developing new skills and competencies in teachers represents another way to accomplish the goal of producing effective learners. One such program, supported in part by the U. S. Office of Education as a component of the Harvard T.T.T. Project, is reported by Mosher and Sprinthall (1971). In this program, doctoral candidates were trained in counseling psychology and curriculum, with the aim of producing educational leaders who would provide the impetus to the establishment of programs to enhance the psychological development of children as a principal component of the modern school. The training program for these potential leaders consisted of five major instructional categories including a critique of the school and its effect on children, the development of counseling skills and strategies in the trainees, a seminar and practicum in teaching, a study of the humanities and their relationship to child growth, and a practicum and seminar on child development.

As Mosher and Sprinthall rather pessimistically put it, the project was developed because ". . . education currently offers little help to adolescents or young adults as people who are trying to mature against unusual vicissitudes. Our objective is to make personal development a central focus of education, rather than a pious rhetoric at commencement, a second-order concern of the English curriculum, or the private guilt of committed teachers and counselors."

We know that student attitudes toward learning, levels of aspiration, self-concept and self-esteem are, to a large degree, products of the educational experience (Jackson, 1968; Mosher and Sprinthall, 1969). The failure to make meaningful changes in school operations and offerings that would enhance personal growth is shared by all educators. However, Mosher and Sprinthall (1971) lay a special responsibility on pupil personnel workers. They say, "one of the principal jobs of psychological personnel in the school is, then, to adjust children to the institution. In so doing, they assume that the school is static, and rarely call into serious question that it may be the school environment that is the 'problem'."

Bardon and Bennett (1974) emphasize the route of modification of teacher skills as a way to enhance the psychological development of children in school. They review such programs as the "C" group method described by Dinkmeyer (1971), human development training (Carkhuff 1971), filial therapy as described by Gerney (1964) and his colleagues, Glasser's (1969) reality therapy, and the "magic circle" technique of Bessell and Palomares (1970). It is interesting to note that all of these, with the exception of the last, are based on approaches to expanding teacher abilities, skills, and understanding, rather than on substantive changes in curriculum, programs, or instructional content.

One manifest development in psychological education has resulted from the interest of the American Psychological Association in the education of children in the behavioral sciences. The Association has received a grant from the National Science Foundation for the development of teaching units in psychology. After six years of preparatory activity, the American Psychological Association in 1974 received a grant of $152,000 for the purpose of developing a series of curriculum materials for instructional use at the high school level. Hopefully, this manifestation of interest on the part of the psychological community will be extended in time to the age level where developmental possibilities for change and growth are most compelling and obvious, namely, the elementary level. At any rate, this action is a positive step in the direction of providing effective psychologically based learning experiences for children.

Making a Choice

No single theory, program, procedure, or body of organized programmatic materials, methods or techniques has emerged with accepted prominence from the various alternatives available in the literature. No dominant plan has succeeded in capturing the interest and imagination of counselors, psychologists and educators. Indeed, the resistance to implementing programs of psychological education in the schools that we discussed earlier in this monograph has, if anything, become more rigid in spite of apparently increased public sensitivity to the affective nature of human beings and its importance in life. Buchholz (1974) maintains that "one thought that scares parents and educators away from handling feelings is the fear of breeding bleeding hearts or tantrum-throwers. On the contrary, true control over feelings comes from being in touch with and accepting the feelings."

This fearfulness to tread "where the angels fear to tread" is coupled with a very real dilemma as to the choice of appropriate educational strategies. Even for the very bold educator who is determined to try to help children in their emotional growth, the matter of developing an instructional program is a very real and formidable obstacle to the implementation of psychological education in the school.

Describing this problem in his brief review of school programs in affective teaching, Mordock (1974) concludes that, "Few of these approaches were based on a developmental conception of children's needs and efforts to evaluate them were minimal. Integration of particular approaches into existing cognitive curriculums was absent and even worse, no real affective curriculum was available for a teacher to follow. . . ." He points out that the DUSO materials and the Ojemann guides (both described earlier in Chapter 3) were the only "organized" programs he had been able to locate.

When will affective learning be regarded as being important as substantive content or as vital as skill acquisition in the schools? Probably not until three conditions are achieved: (1) educators are genuinely convinced that psychological development of the child is as important as cognitive development and that it must be taught just as deliberately as reading and the other content areas, (2) a substantive and accepted integrated theory of cognitive-psychological development of the child is described in necessary depth and breadth, and (3) curriculum structure, program content, and instructional materials and techniques in psycho-education are produced, tested, and validated for teaching use.

It is not clear that the first condition, acceptance of the importance and necessity of psychological education, yet exists in spite of the wealth of authoritative argument that supports it. In an eloquent plea for acceptance of deliberate affective education for children, Torrance (1965) says that "in sudden emergencies, these early-learned strategies for controlling the environment seem to be a major resource. In adaption to stress over time, however, abilities developed through later experiences are called into play." The author maintains that it is a responsibility of the school to aid individuals to master the skills and strategies necessary for coping with predictable stress through educational experiences. Torrance goes on to emphasize that ". . . educators need to understand the psychology of stress and learn how to help children use their personality and mental resources to respond constructively." The very real question is, "can we and will we?"

Lucile Helfat (1973) in her vivid description of a Magic Circle session with children, concludes by paraphrasing the pleas of Lawrence Kubie in his book, *Our Children Today* (1952). His ideas are as pertinent to our consideration today as they were 20 years ago to another group of people who were concerned then about the "whole child."

> The child's fifth freedom is the right to know what he feels. This will require a new set of mores for schools, one which will enable young people from early years to understand and feel and put into words all the hidden things which go on inside them, thus ending a conspiracy of silence with which the development of the child is now distorted both at home and at school. If the conspiracy of silence is to be replaced by the fifth freedom, children must be encouraged and helped to attend to their forbidden thoughts, and to put them into words, i.e., to talk out loud about love and hate and jealousy and fear; about curiosity over the body, and its products and its apertures; about what goes in and what comes out; about what happens inside and what happens outside; about their dim and confused feelings about sex itself; about the strained and stressful relationships within families, which are transplanted into schools. In all of these areas the school must help the children become more articulate.

The most effective strategy for advocates of psychological education to adopt may be the strategy of "incorporation." This strategy would suggest that psychological education would need to lose its identity to gain a viable position in the curriculum structure. By losing its identity and becoming a part of an already accepted content area, it would achieve the twin goals of articulation with established subject matter and enhanced influence on the instructional process generally. There is now some inclination to expand the social studies curriculum to include more emphasis on affective development, and it would seem that this opportunity could be effectively exploited to further the opportunities of children for psychological and affective growth by incorporating behavioral sciences as an integral part of the social studies curriculum. In the final analysis, this strategy may be the only reasonable, realizable, and non-threatening one that can ever be implemented.

Children can learn the principal dynamics of human behavior. Schools can effectively structure materials and experiences to teach these knowledges and translate them into behavioral skills. Finally, children who are taught such skills can function more effectively as students, more productively as citizens, and more happily as human beings. These rather dogmatically stated conclusions are not products of wishful thinking. They are facts that have been substantiated in repeated research findings and demonstrated in life. At this point in time, psychological education for children is a challenge rather than an accomplishment.

BIBLIOGRAPHY

This list contains references to material quoted or summarized in this monograph. It also includes references which were used in researching the topic of psychological education for children. The reader who wishes to pursue the subject further will find many useful sources of information here as well as clues to further research.

Adamson, W. C. A school mental health program: development and design. *Community Mental Health Journal*, 1968, 4, 454–460.

Adler, A. *The problem child*. New York: Capricorn Books, 1963.

Adler, Alfred. *Individual psychology*. (2nd ed.) Totwa, N.J.: Littlefield, 1969.

Alschuler, A. (Ed.) *New directions in psychological education*. Albany, New York: Educational Opportunities Forum, N.Y. State Department of Education, 1969.

Alschuler, A. S. *The achievement motivation development project: A summary and review*. Cambridge, Massachusetts: Harvard Research and Development Center, Graduate School of Education, 1967.

Alschuler, A. S. *How to develop achievement motivation: A manual for teachers*. Middletown, Connecticut: Educational Ventures, Inc., 1969.

Alschuler, A. S. Psychological education. *Journal of Humanistic Psychology*, Spring 1970, 9 (1) 1–16.

American Association for the Advancement of Science, Commission on Science Education. *Preservice science education of elementary school teachers: Guidelines, standards, and recommendations for research and development*. Washington, D.C., 1970.

American Association for Supervision and Curriculum Development. *Learning and mental health in the school*. Yearbook. Washington, D.C., 1966.

American School Health Association, Committee on Mental Health in the Classroom. Mental health in the classroom. *Journal of School Health*, 1968, 38 (May), (entire issue).

American School Health Association, Committee on Mental Health in the Classroom. Suggested areas for guidance in teaching mental health in the classroom. In W. M. Lifton (Ed.) *Educating for tomorrow; the role of media, career, development and society.* New York: Wiley, 1970, 212–229.

Amidon, E. J. and Flanders, N. A. *The role of the teacher in the classroom,* Association for Productive Teaching, 5408 Chicago Avenue, So., Minneapolis, Minn. 55417. (No date)

Anderson, Jo Ann, and Schmidt, W. I. A time for feelings. *Elementary School Guidance and Counseling,* 1967, 1, 47–56.

Anderson, Judith L., Lang, Carol J., and Scott, Virginia R. *Focus on self-development* (Stage One: Awareness; Stage Two: Responding). Chicago: Science Research Associates, Inc., 1970–71.

Association for Supervision and Curriculum Development. *Perceiving, behaving, becoming.* Yearbook NEA, 1962.

Bardon, Jack I. and Bennett, Virginia C. *School psychology.* Englewood Cliffs, N.J.: Prentice-Hall, Inc., 1974.

Barron, Frank. *Creative person and creative process.* New York: Holt, 1969.

Beatty, Walcott H. Emotions — The missing link in education. *Theory and Practice,* 1969, 8 (2), 86–92.

Bennis, W., et al. *Interpersonal dynamics: Essays and readings on human interaction.* Homewood, Illinois: Dorsey Press, 1968.

Bereither, Carl and Engelman, S. *Disadvantaged children in the preschool,* Englewood Cliffs, N.J.: Prentice Hall, 1966.

Berman, Louise M. *New priorities in the curriculum.* Columbus, Ohio: Charles E. Merrill, 1968.

Berne, Eric. *Games people play.* New York: Grove Press, 1964.

Berne, Eric. *Transactional analysis in psychoanalysis.* New York: Grove Press, 1961.

Berger, E. M. The relation between expressed acceptance of self and expressed exceptance of others. *Journal of abnormal social psychology,* 1952, 47, 778–782.

Bessell, H. and Palomares, U. *Methods in human development.* San Diego: Human Development Training Institute, 1967.

Bessell H. and Palomares U. *Methods in human development: Theory manual,* San Diego: Human Development Training Institute, 1970.

Bettelheim, B. *Love is not enough.* New York: Free Press, 1950.

Biber, Barbara. A learning-teaching paradigm integrating intellectual and affective processes. In Bower and Hollister (Eds.), *Behavioral sciences frontiers in education.* New York: Wiley, 1967.

Biber, Barbara. Integration of mental health principles in the school setting. In G. Caplan (Ed.), *Prevention of mental disorders in children.* New York: Basic Books, 1961, pp. 323–352.

Biber, Barbara. *Basic approaches to mental health.* New York: Bank Street College of Education Publications, 1962.

Biber, Barbara. *The psychological impact of school experience.* New York: Bank Street College of Education Publications, 1969.

Bidwell, C. The teacher as a listener — an approach to mental health. *Journal of School Health*, 1967, **37**, 373–383.

Bishop, I. E. and Donovan, A. B. Teaching problem solving as a component of mental health. *Journal of School Health*, 1969, **39**, 411–413.

Bloom, B. (Ed.) *Taxonomy of eductional objectives, Handbook I: Cognitive domain.* New York: David McKay Co., 1956.

Bonney, M. E. *Mental health in education.* Boston: Allyn & Bacon, 1960.

Borton, Terry. What's left behind when school's forgotten? *Saturday Review*, April 19, 1970.

Borton, T. *Reach, touch and teach: Student concerns and process education.* New York: McGraw-Hill, 1970.

Borton, T. Teaching for personal growth: An introduction to new materials. *Mental Hygiene*, 1969, **53**, 594–599.

Bower, E. M. and Hollister, W. (Eds.) *Behavioral science frontiers in education.* New York: Wiley, 1967.

Bower, E. M. Primary prevention of mental and emotional disorders: A frame of reference. In N. Lambert (Ed.), *The protection and promotion of mental health in schools.* (rev. ed.) Public Health Service Mental Health Monograph No. 5. Washington, D.C.: United States Government Printing Office, 1965. pp. 1–9.

Bower, E. M. *Early identification of emotionally handicapped children in school.* Springfield, Ill.: Charles C. Thomas, 1960.

Bower, E. M. On teaching human behavior to humans. *Journal of school psychology*, 1967, **5**, 237–240.

Bower, E. M. (Ed.) *Orthopsychiatry and education.* Detroit, Michigan: Wayne State University Press, 1970.

Bower, E. M. Mental Health. In R. Ebel (Ed.) *Encyclopedia of educational research*, (4th ed.) New York: Macmillan, 1969.

Bower, E. M. Mental health in education (from *Review of educational research* 1962, 32, 441–454) In Harvey F. Clarizio (Ed.) *Mental health and the educative process.* New York: Rand McNally, 1969.

Bovand, E. W., Jr. The psychology of classroom interaction. *Journal of Educational Research.* 1951, **45**, 215–225.

Boy, Angelo & Pine, Gerald. *Expanding the self: Personal growth for teachers.* Dubuque, Iowa: William C. Brown, 1971.

Brown, George I. *Affectivity, classroom climate and teaching.* Washington, D.C.: American Federation of Teachers, 1971, EMS #6.

Brown, George I. Confluent education: Exploring the affective domain. *College Board Review*, Summer 1971, **80**, 4–10.

Brown, George I. *Human teaching for human learning.* New York: Viking Press, 1971.

Bruner, Jerome S. *The process of education.* New York: Alfred A. Knopf, 1963.

Bruce, P. Relationship of self acceptance of other variables with 6th grade children oriented in self-understanding, *Journal of Educational Psychology,* 1958, **49**, 229.

Buchholz, Ester S. The proper study for children: Children and their feelings: *Psychology in the Schools,* 1974, **11** (1), 10–15.

Bugental, J. *Challenges of humanistic psychology.* New York: McGraw-Hill, 1967.

Bullis, Edmund H., and O'Malley, Faith E. *Human relations in the classroom. Course I.* Wilmington: Delaware State Society for Mental Hygiene, 1957.

Burgess, B. A. *A bibliography: Compiled for a human development curriculum.* Philadelphia: The Intensive Learning Center, The School District of Philadelphia, 1969.

Burnes, A. J. Laboratory instruction in the behavioral sciences in the grammar school. In B. Gertz (Ed.), *Behavioral sciences in the elementary grades.* Cambridge, Mass.: Lesley College, Second Annual Graduate Symposium, 1966. pp. 14–25.

Canfield, J. *A guide to humanistic education.* San Francisco: (No date) Association of Humanistic Psychology.

Canfield, J. T. *Affective, humanistic and psychological education: A basic bibliography.* Amherst: Center for Humanistic Education, University of Mass., 1970.

Caplan, G. (Ed.) *Prevention of mental disorders in children.* New York: Basic Books, 1961.

Carkhuff, R. and Truax, C. Lay mental health counseling, *Journal of consulting psychology,* 1965, **12**, 29, & 426–431.

Carkhuff, R. R. *The development of human resources: Education, psychology and social change.* New York: Holt, Rinehart and Winston, 1971.

Carkhuff, R. R. *Helping and human relations, Vol. I & II.* New York: Holt, Rinehart & Winston, 1969.

Carter, R. *Help! These kids are driving me crazy!* Champaign, Illinois: Research Press, 1972.

Christensen, C. M. Relationships between pupil achievement, pupil affect-need, teacher warmth and teacher permissiveness. *Journal of Educational Psychology,* 1960, **51** (3), 169–174.

Clarizio, H. F. (Ed.) *Mental health and the educative process: Selected readings.* Chicago: Rand McNally, 1969.

Combs, Arthur W. and Snygg, Donald, *Individual behavior.* New York: Harper & Brothers, 1959.

Cianciola, Patricia, Children's literature can affect coping behavior. *Personnel and Guidance Journal,* May 1965, 897–903.

Cowen, E. L. et al. *Emergent approaches to mental health problems.* New York: Appleton-Century-Crofts, 1967.

Dewey, John. *Experience and education.* New York: MacMillan, 1963.

Dinkmeyer, D., The "C" group: Integrating knowledge and experience to change behavior — an Adlerian approach to consultation. *The Counseling Psychologist,* 1971, **3** & 63–72.

Dinkmeyer, D. *Developing Understanding of Self and Others,* Circle Pines, Minnesota: American Guidance Service, Inc., 1970.

Dinkmeyer, Don and Ogburn, K. D. Psychologists' priorities: Premium on developing understanding of self and others. *Psychology in the Schools,* 1974, **9** (1), 24–27.

Doll, R. C. and Fleming, R. S. *Children under pressure.* Columbus, Ohio: Charles E. Merrill, 1966.

Dow, Peter. Human behavior, *The School Psychology Digest,* Summer 1972, **1** (3), 39–41 (Condensed from *Nations schools,* 1971, **88** (2), 38–41 by Marvin S. Kaplan.)

Drews, E. M. Beyond curriculum. *Journal of Humanistic Psychology,* 1968, **8** (2), 9–12.

Dusek, J. B. Implications of development theory for child mental health. *American Psychologist,* 1974, **29** (1), 19–24.

Elliott, L. H. Teaching for life adjustment. *Elementary School Journal,* 1950, **51**, 152–256.

Ellis, A. *Reason and emotion in psychotherapy.* New York: Lyle Stuart, 1962.

Ellis, A. *Growth through Reason.* Palo Alto: Science and Behavior Books, 1971.

English, Horace B. Education of the emotions. *Journal of Humanistic Psychology,* 1961, **1** (9), 101–109.

Feldman, R. and Coppersmith, S. *A resource and reference bibliography in early childhood education and developmental psychology. The affective domain* Washington, D.C.: Office of Child Development, USDHEW. 1969.

Freed, Alvyn M., *Transational analysis for kids and grown-ups, too.* Sacramento, California: Jalmar Press, Inc., 1971.

Gearing, F. O. Toward a mankind curriculum. *Today's Education,* 1970, **59** (3) 28–30.

Gerney, B. G. *Psychotherapeutic agents: New roles for nonprofessionals, parents and teachers.* New York: Holt & Rinehart, 1964.

Gibson, J. S. *The inter-group relations curriculum: A program for elementary school education,* Medford, Mass.: Tufts University Press, 1969.

Gillham, Helen. *Helping children accept themselves and others.* New York: Columbia University Bureau of Publications, 1959.

Ginott, H. C. *Between parent and child: New solutions to old problems.* New York: MacMillan, 1967.

Ginott, H. C. *Between parent and teenager.* New York: MacMillan, 1969.

Glasser, W. *Reality therapy: A new approach to psychiatry.* New York: Harper & Row, 1965.

Glasser, W. *Schools without failure.* New York: Harper & Row, 1969.

Gordon, Ira J. Affect and cognition: A reciprocal relationship. *Educational Leadership,* April 1970, 661–664.

Gordon, Richard and Gordon, Katherine. *The blight on the ivy.* Englewood Cliffs, New Jersey: Prentice-Hall, 1963, p. 8.

Gordon, Thomas. *Parent effectiveness training.* New York: Peter H. Wyden Publishers, 1970.

Gordon, W. J. *Synectics: The development of creative capacity.* New York: Harper & Row, 1961.

Greenberg, Herbert M. *Teaching with feeling: Compassion and self-awareness in the classroom today.* New York: MacMillan, 1968.

Grunwald, Bernice. Role playing as a classroom group procedure. *The Individual Psychologist,* 1969, 6 (2), 34–38.

Grussi, Robert. "The Telephone Game," "Self Searching," and the "Blind and Silent Walk." mimeographed paper dated May 12, 1972.

Hamachek, Don E. Self-concept as related to motivation and learning, *Motivation in teaching and learning; What research says to the teacher,* Washington, D.C.: Association of Classroom Teachers, NEA, 1969.

Harlow, Harry F. *Learning to love.* New York: Ballantine, 1973.

Harris, Tom. *I'm OK, You're OK,* New York: Harper & Row, 1967.

Heath, Douglas H. *Humanizing schools.* New York: Hayden Book Co., 1971.

Hefferman, Helen. Challenge or pressure. In Ronald C. Doll and Robert S. Fleming (Eds.), *Children under pressure.* Columbus, Ohio: Charles E. Merrill, Inc., 1966.

Helfat, Lucile. The gut-level needs of kids. *Learning: The magazine for creative teaching.* Palo Alto, California: Education Today Co., October 1973.

Henderson, G. and Bibens, R. F. *Teachers should care: Social perspective of teaching.* New York: Harper & Row, 1970.

Hollingshed, A. B. and Redlick, R. C. *Social class and mental illness: A community study.* New York: John Wiley and Sons, 1958.

Hollister, W. G. An overview of school mental health activities. *Journal of School Health,* 1966, 36, 114–117.

Hollister, W. G. Current trends in mental health programming in the classroom. *Journal of social issues,* 1959, 15, 50–58.

Home-School-Community system for child development. NIMH Grant #ROI MH 16666-OIAX, Atlanta City Schools, 1973.

Holt, John. *How children fail.* New York: Delta, 1966.

Holt, John. *What do I do Monday?* New York: Dutton, 1970.

Huxley, Aldous. Education on the nonverbal level. *Daedalus,* 1962, **91** (2), 279–293.

Ivey, Allen E. and Alschuler, Alfred S. An introduction to the field. *Personnel and Guidance Journal.* 1973, **51** (9), 594.

Jackson, P. *Life in the classroom.* New York: Holt, Rinehart and Winston, 1968.

Jahoda, Marie. *Current concepts of positive mental health.* New York: Basic Jersild, A. *In search of self.* New York: Teachers College Press, 1954.

Jersild, Arthur. *When teachers face themselves.* New York: Teachers College Press, 1955.

Jersild, A. T. and Helfant, K. *Education for self-understanding: The roles of psychology in the high school program.* New York: Teachers College, Columbia University, 1953.

Jones, R. M. *Fantasy and feelings in education.* New York: Harper and Row, 1970.

Joint Commission on Mental Health of Children. *Mental health: From infancy through adolescence, reports of Task Forces I, II, and III and the Committee on Education and Religion.* New York: Harper & Row, 1973. pp. 80, 137–138.

Jourard, S. *Disclosing man to himself:* Princeton, New Jersey: Van Nostrand, 1968.

Kaplan, Louis. *Education and mental health.* New York: Harper & Row, January, 1971.

Kelley, Earl. *Education for what is real.* New York: Harper & Row, 1947.

Kelley, E. C. How the high school can educate for human understanding. *School review,* 1949, pp. 57, 353–357.

Kelley, Earl C. The place of affective learning. *Educational Leadership,* 1965, pp. 22, 455–457.

Kirk, S. A. *Educatiing exceptional children.* (2nd ed.) Boston: Houghton Mifflin, 1972, pp. 183–186.

Kirschenbaum, H. A., Simon, S. and Napier, R. W. *Wad-Ja-Get? The grading game in American education.* New York: Hart, 1971.

Kohl, H. R. *Thirty-six children.* New York: New American Library, 1967.

Krathwohl, David R., Bloom, Benjamin S., and Masia, Bertram B. *Taxonomy of educational objectives, Handbook II: The affective domain.* New York: McKay, 1964.

Krathwohl, D. R., Bloom, B. S. and Masia, B. B. *Taxonomy of educational objectives: The classification of educational goals.* New York: McKay, 1964.

Krumboltz, J. D. and Krumboltz, H. *Changing children's behavior.* Englewood Cliffs, New Jersey: Prentice-Hall, 1972.

Kubie, Lawrence. *Our children today.* New York: Viking Press, 1952.

Lambert, N. (Ed.) *The protection and promotion of mental health in schools.* Public Health Service Mental Health Monograph, No. 6, Washington, D.C.: United States Government Printing Office, 1965.

Lederman, J. *Anger and the rocking chair.* New York: McGraw-Hill, 1969.

Levine, Esther. Affective education: Lessons in ego development. *Psychology in the Schools,* 1973, **10** (2), 147–150.

Limbacher, W. J. An approach to elementary training in mental health. *Journal of School Psychology,* 1967, **5** (3), 225–234.

Lombardo, A. A mental health curriculum for the lower grades. *Mental Hygiene,* 1968, **52,** 570–576.

Long, B. E. Behavioral science for elementary school pupils. *Elementary School Journal,* 1970, **70,** 253–260.

Long, B. E. A model for elementary school behavioral science as an agent of primary prevention. *American Psychologist,* 1970, **25,** 571–574.

Long, B. E. *Journey to myself.* Austin, Texas: Steck-Vaughn Co., (in press).

Long, B. To teach about human behavior. *Educational leadership,* 1970, 27, 683–685.

Long, B. E. Why do people do what they do. *Grade Teacher.* April, 1972 pp. 70–72.

Long, B. E. *Ideas for people watching.* Herder & Herder. (In Press)

Lyon, Harold C. Humanistic education for the whole man. *Learning to feel — Feeling to learn.* Columbus, Ohio: Charles C. Merrill, 1971.

Malamud, D. I. and Maschover, S. *Toward self-understanding: Group techniques in self-confrontation.* Springfield, Illinois: Charles C. Thomas, 1965.

Manning, Duane. *Toward a humanistic curriculum.* New York: Harper & Row, 1971.

Maslow, A. *Motivation and personality.* New York: Harper & Row, 1954. (2nd Ed., 1970).

Maslow, Abraham H. Some educational implications of the humanistic psychologies. *Harvard Educational Review,* 1968, **38** (4), 685–96.

May , R. *Love and will.* New York: Norton, 1969.

McCandless, Boyd R. *Children: Behavior and development.* (2nd ed.) New York: Holt, Rinehart and Winston, Inc., 1967.

Miel, A. and Brogan, P. *More than social studies: a view of social learning in the elementary school.* Englewood Cliffs, New Jersey: Prentice-Hall, 1957.

Miller, G. Dean. *Additional studies in elementary school guidance: Psychological education activities evaluated.* St. Paul: Minnesota Department of Education, 1973.

Minuchin, P. Biber, B., Shapiro, E. and Zimiles, H. *The psychological impact of school experience: A comparative study of nine-year old children in contrasting schools.* New York: Basic Books, 1969.

Montessori, Marie. *Dr. Montessori's own handbook.* New York: Schocken Books, 1965.

Mordock, John B. Affective education: Where to Begin? *The School Psychologist,* 1974, **27** (3), 6.

Mosah, H. H. Strategies for behavior change in schools: Consultation strategies — A personal account. *The Counseling Psychologist,* 1971, **3** (1), 58–62.

Mosher, Ralph and Sprinthall, Norman A. *Studies of adolescents in the secondary school.* Monograph 6, Cambridge, Mass.: Center for Research and Development. Harvard Graduate School of Education, 1969.

Mosher, Ralph and Sprinthall, Norman A. Psychological education: A means to promote personal development during adolescense. *The Counseling Psychologist.* 1971, **2** (4).

Moustakas, Clark E. *The teacher and the child: Personal interaction in the classroom.* New York: McGraw-Hill, 1956.

Moustakas, C. E. *The authentic teacher: Sensitivity and awareness in the classroom.* Cambridge, Massachusetts: H. A. Doyle, 1966.

Nash, Paul. Integrating feeling, thinking and acting in teacher education. *AACTE Bulletin.* April 1971, **24** (2), 7–8.

Neill, A. S. *Freedom not license.* New York: Hart, 1966.

Noland, R. L. and Bardon, J. I. Supplementary bibliography on teaching psychology and the behavioral sciences in the schools. *Journal of School Psychology,* 1967, **5**, 257–260.

Ojemann, R. H. Investigations on the effects of teaching an understanding and appreciation of behavior dynamics. In G. Caplan (Ed.). *Prevention of mental disorders in children.* New York: Basic Books, 1961, pp. 378–396.

Ojemann, R. H. Incorporating psychological concepts in the school curriculum. *Journal of School Psychology,* 1967, **5**, 195–204.

Ojemann, R. H. Incorporating psychological concepts in the school curriculum *Journal of school psychology,* 1967, 5, 195–204.

Ojemann, R. H. et al. *Education in human behavior: Handbook for first grade teachers.* Cleveland: Educational Research Council of America, 1961.

Ojemann, R. H. *Developing a program for education in human behavior.* Cleveland: Educational Research Council of America, 1972.

Ojemann, R. H. *The causal approach to human behavior through literature.* Cleveland: Educational Research Council of America, 1970.

Ojemann, Ralph. Education in human behavior in perspective. *People watching.* New York: Behavioral Publications, 1972, 1 (2), 58–67.

Ojemann, Ralph. Brief description of the program of education in human behavior and potential. Cleveland: Educational Research Council of America, 1972.

Otto, H. A. *A guide to developing your potential.* New York: Charles Scribner, 1971.

Parnes, S. J. *Creative behavior guidebook*. New York: Charles Scribner, 1967.

People watching: New York: Behavioral Publications, periodical.

Pfeiffer, J. W. and Heslin, R. *Instrumentation in human relations training.* Iowa City: University Associates Publishing Company, 1973.

Prescott, Daniel A. *Emotion and the educative process*. Washington, D.C.: American Council on Education, 1938.

Prescott, Daniel A. *The child in the educative process*. New York: McGraw-Hill, 1957.

PROJECT DIRECT. *Guidance learning handbook*. Title III, Elementary and Secondary Education Act. Georgia State Department of Education, 1969.

Randolph, N. and Howe, W. *Self-enhancing education*. Palo Alto, California: Educational Development Corporation. 1966.

Riessman, Frank, Cohen, Jerome and Pearl, Arthur. *Mental health of the poor.* New York: The Free Press of Glenco, 1964.

Roen, S. R. The behavioral sciences in the primary grades. *American Psychologist*, 1965, **20**, 43–432.

Roen, S. R. Behavioral studies as a curriculum subject. *Teachers College Record*. 1967, **68**, 541–550.

Roen, S. R. Primary prevention in the classroom through a teaching program in the behavioral sciences. In E. L. Cowen, E. A. Gardner, and M. Zaz (Eds.) *Emergent approaches to mental health problems*. New York: Appleton-Century-Crofts, 1967, pp. 252–270.

Roen, S. R. Teaching the behavioral sciences in elementary grades. *Journal of School Psychology,* 1967, **5**, 205–216.

Roen, S. R. Relevance of teaching children about behavior. *American Journal of Orthopsychiatry.* 1970, **40**, 307–308.

Roen, S. R. Teaching behavioral science in the elementary school classroom. *The encyclopedia of education*. New York: MacMillan, 1971.

Roen, S. R. References to *Teaching children about human behavior: Pre-high school, A Bibliography*. New York: Teachers College, Columbia University, NIMH Grant #1ROIMH 17554-01JP.

Rogers, C. R. *Client-centered therapy: Its current practice, implications and theory*. Boston: Houghton Mifflin, 1951.

Rogers, C. R. *Freedom to learn*. Columbus, Ohio: Charles E. Merrill, 1970.

Rogers, C. R. Mental health findings in three elementary schools. *Educational Research Bulletin,* 1942, **21**, 86–91.

Rogers, Dorothy. *Mental hygiene in elementary education*. Boston: Houghton Mifflin, 1957, p. 5, 6.

Sanford, Nevitt. The development of cognitive-affective processes through education. In E. M. Bower and W. Hollister (Eds.) *Behavioral science frontiers in education*. New York: Wiley, 1967.

Sax, Sanville and Hollander, Sandra. *Reality games.* New York: MacMillan, 1972.

Schell, John S. Curriculum for teacher preparation for teachers of elementary and high school psychology courses. *Journal of School Psychology,* 1967, **5** (3), 191–194.

Scobey, M. M. and Graham, G. (Eds.) *To nurture humaneness: Commitment for the 70's.* Washington: Association for Supervision and Curriculum Development, 1970.

Sewell, L. *Educating for success.* Queens College (in press).

Shertzer, Bruce and Stone, Shelley C. *Fundmentals of guidance.* (2nd ed.) Boston: Houghton Mifflin, 1971.

Shulman, J. L., Ford, R. C. and Busk, Patricia. A classroom program to improve self-concept. *Psychology in the Schools,* 1973, **10** (4), 487.

Solvertz, F. and Lund, Alice. Some effects of a personal developmental program at the fifth grade level. *Journal of Educational Research,* 1956, **49,** 373–378.

Stiles, Frances S. A study of materials and programs for developing an understanding of behavior at the elementary school level. Unpublished doctoral dissertation, State University of Iowa, 1947.

Tanner, Laurel N. and Lendgren, H. C. *Classroom teaching and learning: A Mental Health Approach.* New York: Holt, 1971.

The School Counselor, May 1973, 20 (5). Special Feature: Psychological Education.

Torrance, E. Paul and Myers, R. E. *Creative learning and teaching.* New York: Dodd, Mead & Co., 1970.

Torrance, E. Paul *Encouraging creativity in the classroom.* Dubuque, Iowa: William C. Brown, 1971.

Torrance, E. Paul *Mental health and constructive behavior.* Belmont, California: Wadsworth Publishing Co., Inc., 1965.

Trow, W. C. Psychology and the behavioral sciences in the schools. *Journal of School Psychology,* 1967, **5,** 241–249.

Truax, C. B. and Tatum, C. R. An extension from the effective psychotherapeutic model to constructive personality change in pre-school children. *Childhood Education,* 1966, **42** (7), 456–462.

Waetjen, W. B. and Leeper, R. R. (Eds.) *Learning and mental health in the schools.* Washington, D.C.: Association for Supervision and Curriculum Development, 1966.

Wagner, Anna. *Sharing my world: A course in human/personal development for elementary children.* New York: Vantage Press, 1974.

Weinstein, Gerald and Fantini, Mario. *Toward humanistic education: A curriculum of affect.* New York: Praeger, 1970.

Whiteman, M. Children's conceptions of psychological causality. *Child Development,* 1967, **1,** 141–155.

Wiles, K. *The changing curriculum of the American high school.* Englewood Cliffs, New Jersey: Prentice-Hall, 1963.

Wilhelms, Fred T. *The ungovernable curriculum.* Paper given to the council of Chief State School Officers, Portland, Oregon, August 1972.

Wilson, F. M. *Mental health in the intermediate grades, mental health in modern education.* Yearbook: National Society for the Study of Education, Chicago: University of Chicago Press, 1954, p. 196.

Valett, Robert E. *Affective-humanistic education: Goals, programs and learning activities.* Belmont, California: Fearon Publishers, 1974.

Valett, Robert E. *Getting it all together.* San Rafael, California: Academic Therapy, 1974.

INDEX

4232016